Daily
Academic Vocabulary

GRADE 4

Editorial Development: Bonnie Brook
Communications
Content Editing: Marilyn Evans
Leslie Sorg
Copy Editing: Sonny Bennett
Art Direction: Cheryl Puckett
Cover Design: Cheryl Puckett
Illustration: Jim Palmer
Design/Production: Carolina Caird
Arynne Elfenbein

EMC 2760

Evan-Moor.
Helping Children Learn

Visit
teaching-standards.com
to view a correlation
of this book.
This is a free service.

Correlated to State Standards

**Congratulations on your purchase of some of the
finest teaching materials in the world.**

*Photocopying the pages in this book
is permitted for <u>single-classroom use only</u>.
Making photocopies for additional classes
or schools is prohibited.*

Contents

About Academic Vocabulary

What Is Academic Vocabulary?

Academic vocabulary is that critical vocabulary that students meet again and again in their reading and classroom work across all content areas. Feldman and Kinsella refer to these high-use, widely applicable words—words such as *compare*, *occurrence*, *structure*, *sequential*, *symbolize*, and *inference*—as "academic tool kit words."[1]

Why Is Academic Vocabulary Instruction Important?

Vocabulary knowledge is one of the most reliable predictors of academic success. Studies show a major difference over time between the achievement levels of children who enter school with a strong oral vocabulary and those who begin their schooling with a limited vocabulary. Dr. Anita Archer says, "In many ways the 'Reading Gap,' especially after second and third grade, is essentially a Vocabulary Gap—and the longer students are in school the wider the gap becomes."[2] Focused vocabulary instruction can reduce this gap.

Knowing academic vocabulary—the "vocabulary of learning"—is essential for students to understand concepts presented in school. Yet academic English is not typically part of students' natural language and must be taught. "One of the most crucial services that teachers can provide, particularly for students who do not come from academically advantaged backgrounds, is systematic instruction in important academic terms."[3]

What Does Research Say About Vocabulary Instruction?

Common practices for teaching vocabulary—looking up words in the dictionary, drawing meaning from context, and impromptu instruction—are important but cannot be depended upon alone to develop the language students need for academic success.

Most vocabulary experts recommend a comprehensive vocabulary development program with direct instruction of important words. *Daily Academic Vocabulary* utilizes direct teaching in which students use academic language in speaking, listening, reading, and writing. Used consistently, *Daily Academic Vocabulary* will help students acquire the robust vocabulary necessary for academic success.

[1]Feldman, K., and Kinsella, K. "Narrowing the Language Gap: The Case for Explicit Vocabulary Instruction." New York: Scholastic, 2004.
[2]Archer, A. "Vocabulary Development." Working paper, 2003. (http://www.fcoe.net/ela/pdf/Anita%20Archer031.pdf)
[3]Marzano, R. J. and Pickering, D. J. *Building Academic Vocabulary*. Alexandria, VA: Association for Supervision and Curriculum Development, 2005.

Tips for Successful Vocabulary Teaching

The "Weekly Walk-Through" on pages 6 and 7 presents a suggested instructional path for teaching the words in *Daily Academic Vocabulary*. Here are some ideas from vocabulary experts to ensure that students get the most from these daily lessons.*

Active Participation Techniques

- Active participation means ALL students are speaking and writing.
- Use **choral responses**:
  - Pronounce the word together.
  - Read the sentence/question together.
  - Complete cloze sentences together.
- Use **nonverbal responses**:
  - Students give thumbs-up signal, point to the word, etc.
  - Make sure students wait for your signal to respond.
- Use **partner responses**:
  - Have students practice with a partner first.
  - Listen in on several pairs.
- Allow thinking time before taking responses.
- Randomly call on students; don't ask for raised hands.
- Ask students to rephrase what a partner or other classmate said.

Model and Practice

- Use an oral cloze strategy when discussing a new word. Invite choral responses. For example: *If I read you the end of a story, I am reading you the _____.* (Students say, "conclusion.")
- Complete the open-ended sentence (activity 1 on Days 1–4) yourself before asking students to do so.
- Make a point of using the week's words in your conversation and instruction (both oral and written). Be sure to call students' attention to the words and confirm understanding in each new context.
- Encourage students to look for the week's words as they read content area texts.
- Find moments during the day (waiting in line, in between lessons) to give students additional opportunities to interact with the words. For example:

  *If what I say is an example of **accomplish**, say "accomplish." If what I say is <u>not</u> an example of **accomplish**, show me a thumbs-down sign.*

  > *I meant to clean my room, but I watched TV instead.* (thumbs down)
  > *Stacia read two books a week, more than any other student.* ("accomplish")
  > *The scientists found a cure for the disease.* ("accomplish")
  > *The mechanic could not fix our car.* (thumbs down)

* See also page 9 for specific ideas for English language learners.

Weekly Walk-Through

Each week of *Daily Academic Vocabulary* follows the same five-day format, making the content more accessible for both students and teacher.

Using the reproducible definitions and the teacher lesson plan page, follow the instructional steps below to introduce each day's word or words.

1. **Pronounce** the word and point out the part of speech. Then have students say the word with you several times. If the word is long, pronounce it again by syllables, having students repeat after you.

2. **Read the definition** of the word; paraphrase using simpler or different language if necessary.

3. **Read the example sentence** and then have students read it with you. Discuss how the word is used in the sentence and ask questions to confirm understanding. For example: *We are waiting for a* **definite** *answer from Aunt Caitlin about when she is coming for a visit.* Ask: *What kind of answer would be a* **definite** *answer? What kind of answer would <u>not</u> be a* **definite** *answer?* Provide additional example sentences as necessary.

4. **Elaborate** on the meaning of the word using the suggestions on the teacher lesson plan page. These suggestions draw on common life experiences to illustrate the word meaning and give students opportunities to generate their own examples of use.

Teacher Resources

Reproducible Definitions

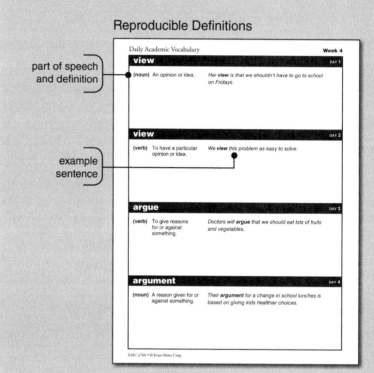

Teacher Lesson Plan

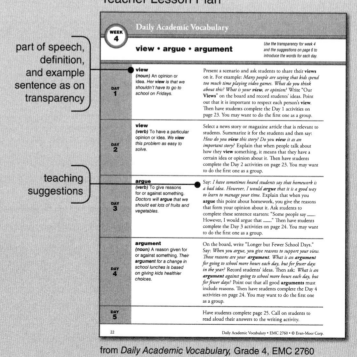

from *Daily Academic Vocabulary*, Grade 4, EMC 2760

Daily Academic Vocabulary • EMC 2760 • © Evan-Moor Corp.

Student Practice Pages

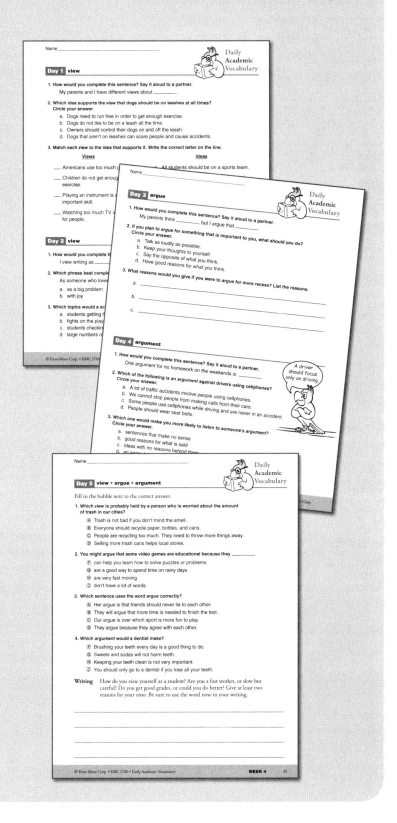

5. **Assess** students' understanding of the word(s) with the reproducible activities for Days 1 through 4.

The first item is always an oral activity that is designed to be open-ended and answerable based on personal experience. You may wish to model a response before asking students to complete the item. Make sure that all students respond orally. Then call on a number of students to share their responses or those of a partner.

Until students become familiar with the variety of formats used in the daily practice, you may wish to do the activities together as a class. This will provide support for English language learners and struggling readers.

6. **Review and assess** mastery of all the words from the week on Day 5. The review contains four multiple-choice items and a writing activity requiring students to use one or more of the week's words.

The instructional steps above were modeled after those presented by Kevin Feldman, Ed.D. and Kate Kinsella, Ed.D. in "Narrowing the Language Gap: The Case for Explicit Vocabulary Instruction," Scholastic Inc., 2004.

Review Week Walk-Through

Weeks 9, 18, 27, and 36 are review weeks. Each review covers all the words from the previous eight weeks.

Days 1–4

On Day 1 through Day 4 of the review weeks, students determine which academic vocabulary words complete a cloze paragraph.

Day 5

Day 5 of the review weeks alternates between a crossword puzzle and a crack-the-code puzzle.

Teacher Page

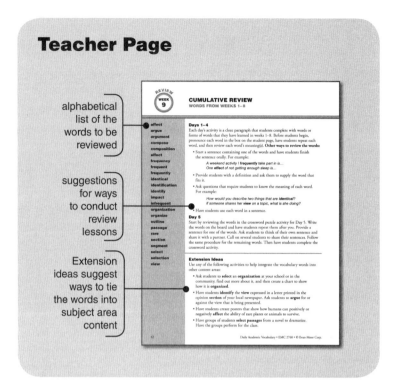

Student Practice Pages

Days 1–4

Day 5

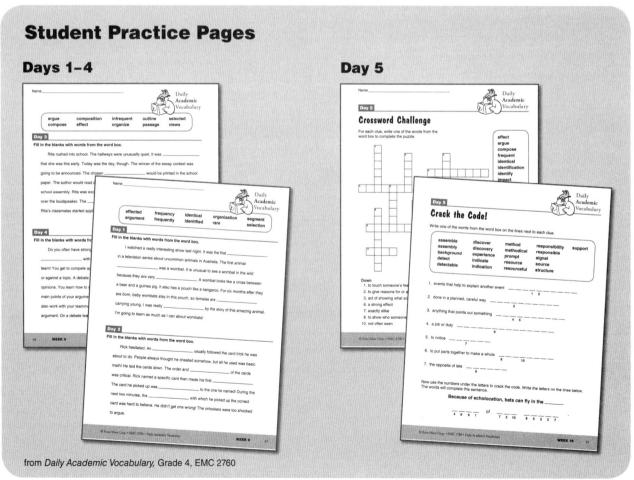

from *Daily Academic Vocabulary*, Grade 4, EMC 2760

Meeting the Needs of English Language Learners

In addition to the direct, scaffolded instruction presented in *Daily Academic Vocabulary*, you may want to use some of the following sheltering strategies to assist English language learners in accessing the vocabulary.

Use Graphics
Draw a picture, a symbol, or other graphics such as word or idea maps to represent the word. Keep it simple. Then ask students to draw their own pictures. For example:

categorize   **similar**

Use Cognates with Spanish-Speaking Students
Cognates—words that are similar in meaning, spelling, and pronunciation—can make English more accessible for Spanish speakers. There are thousands of English words that have a related Spanish word. For example:

typical	típico
variety	variedad
combination	combinación

Model Correct Syntax and Usage in Oral Discussions
Model correct pronunciation. Use echoing strategies to teach correct usage and syntax. Teach the varied forms of words together, *agree* and *agreement* for example, to help students understand correct usage.

Provide Sentence Frames
For written activities, such as the final activity on all Day 5 pages, provide sentence starters or sentence frames that students can complete. For example:

*We knew that our study method was **effective** because…*

Teach Communication Strategies
Engaging in academic discussions requires a more formal language. Teach a variety of ways to begin responses when reporting or asking questions in class. For example:

Change this	To this
My partner said…	My partner shared/pointed out/indicated that…
That's not right!	I don't agree with you because…
I don't get it.	Will you explain that to me again?

compose • composition

Use the reproducible definitions on page 160 and the suggestions on page 6 to introduce the words for each day.

DAY 1

compose
(verb) To be the parts of something; make up. *Six small squares* **compose** *the large rectangle.*

Use six sticky notes to demonstrate the sample sentence by sticking them on the board to create a rectangle. Say: *I am using these squares to make up a new shape: a rectangle. The squares now* **compose** *a rectangle.* Have students locate things in the classroom that can be described as being **composed** of parts. Have students use the sentence starter, "(Object) is **composed** of...." Then have students complete the Day 1 activities on page 11. You may want to do the first one as a group.

DAY 2

composition
(noun) What something is made of. *The* **composition** *of our class is more girls than boys.*

Bring in a bowl of flour and a pitcher of water to create paste. Say: *I am going to make paste. The* **composition** *of it calls for equal parts of water and flour. The* **composition** *of something is the parts that make it up.* While you work, ask students to explain the **composition** of other basic mixtures such as sea water (water and salt) or mud (dirt and water). Encourage students to use the word **composition** in their explanations. Then have students complete the Day 2 activities on page 11. You may want to do the first one as a group.

DAY 3

compose
(verb) To write or create. *You should* **compose** *a thank-you note after receiving a gift.*

Say: *Writers compose stories; songwriters* **compose** *songs. They create, or* **compose**, *their works for a living.* Ask students to name things that they have recently **composed**. (e.g., a letter; an essay; a poem; a speech) Ask them to use the sentence starter, "I have **composed** a ___." Then have students complete the Day 3 activities on page 12. You may want to do the first one as a group.

DAY 4

composition
(noun) A musical or written work, such as a song or essay. *Her* **composition** *won first prize in the state essay contest.*

Say: *If I compose a song, I have created a* **composition**. *If you write an essay, or a piece of writing on one topic, that is also called a* **composition**. Ask: *Have you created* **compositions**? *What topics have you created* **compositions** *on?* Encourage students to use the word **composition** in their responses. Then have students complete the Day 4 activities on page 12. You may want to do the first one as a group.

DAY 5

Have students complete page 13. Call on students to read aloud their answers to the writing activity.

Daily Academic Vocabulary

Day 1 compose

1. How would you complete this sentence? Say it aloud to a partner.

Schools are composed of _____.

2. Which things might a sand castle be *composed* of? Circle your answer.

a. bird, fish, person

b. sand, water, shells

c. shovel, cup, bucket

d. beach, ocean, sun

3. What ingredients *compose* your favorite pizza? List the toppings.

My Favorite Pizza:

Topping #1 _____

Topping #2 _____

Topping #3 _____

Topping #4 _____

Day 2 composition

1. How would you complete this sentence? Say it aloud to a partner.

The composition of our class includes _____.

2. Which list shows the *composition* of a popular fruit drink? Circle your answer.

a. pitcher, ice, glass

b. hot milk, chocolate

c. hot water, spices, milk

d. lemon juice, water, sugar

3. Which list describes the *composition* of a library? Circle your answer.

a. writing, reading, homework, study

b. books, magazines, shelves, tables

c. big, quiet, busy, crowded

d. cover, pages, index, title

Day 3 compose

1. How would you complete this sentence? Say it aloud to a partner.

If I could compose a song, it would be about _____.

2. Which one would you not compose? Circle your answer.

a. letter   c. flute

b. essay   d. story

3. Match the things you *compose* to what they might include.
   Write the correct letter on the line.

____ poem   a. plot

____ letter   b. rhyming words

____ song   c. musical notes

____ story   d. address

Day 4 composition

1. How would you complete this sentence? Say it aloud to a partner.

The first thing I do when creating a composition is _____.

2. Which contest would call for *compositions* as entries? Circle your answer.

a. Cookie Bake-Off   c. Pet Show Parade

b. Best Young Writers Competition   d. Science Fair Experiment

3. Which *composition* has these parts: introduction, body, conclusion? Circle your answer.

a. sculpture   c. poem

b. painting   d. essay

4. Briefly summarize the last *composition* you wrote.

_____

_____

_____

Day 5 compose • composition

Fill in the bubble next to the correct answer.

1. Grapes, bananas, pears, and apples can *compose* a _____.

    Ⓐ tree

    Ⓑ jar of jelly

    Ⓒ fruit basket

    Ⓓ song

2. Why would scientists study the *composition* of rocks?

    Ⓕ to see what they are made of

    Ⓖ to make paper

    Ⓗ to predict the weather

    Ⓙ to break them apart easily

3. Why would you *compose* an advertisement?

    Ⓐ to express your feelings

    Ⓑ to see what is on sale

    Ⓒ to show your musical talent

    Ⓓ to try to sell something

4. Which sentence uses the word *composition* correctly?

    Ⓕ The class needed to composition a poster for the event.

    Ⓖ A good writer does more than one draft of a composition.

    Ⓗ Our composition tastes good.

    Ⓙ I often composition my ideas in pencil first.

Writing   Describe your favorite meal. Be sure to use the word *compose* or *composition* in your description.

_____

_____

_____

_____

organize • organization

Use the reproducible definitions on page 161 and the suggestions on page 6 to introduce the words for each day.

DAY 1

organize
(verb) To put together in a neat and orderly way. *I organize my clothes by type and color.*

organization
(noun) The way in which things are arranged or grouped together. *The organization of the books is by author, not by subject.*

Say: *We are going to organize what you do every day using a diagram.* Draw a Venn diagram on the board. Above one circle, write "School," and above the other, "Home." Ask: *What are things you only do at school? What are things you only do at home? What are things you do at both places?* Say: *The Venn diagram shows the organization of your activities.* Ask: *What else do you organize? What is the organization of those things? How does the organization help you?* Encourage students to use the words **organize** and **organization** in their responses. Then have students complete the Day 1 activities on page 15. You may want to do the first one as a group.

DAY 2

organize
(verb) To plan and run an event. *Scout troops organize a big cookie sale every year.*

Ask: *If I were to organize a field trip to a museum, what would I need to do?* (e.g., get bus; lunches; tickets) Say: *It takes a lot of work to organize an event.* Ask: *Have you ever helped to organize an event? What was it?* Then have students complete the Day 2 activities on page 15. You may want to do the first one as a group.

DAY 3

organize
(verb) To join together, or form, a group of people. *The players will organize a new soccer team this summer.*

Have students raise their hands if their birthday is in the summer. Say: *I plan to organize the Summer Birthday Club, and I would like you to be the members of the club.* Explain to students that people can be **organized** into groups if they share interests (such as soccer) or have a connection to each other (such as birthdays). Then have students complete the Day 3 activities on page 16. You may want to do the first one as a group.

DAY 4

organization
(noun) A group of people joined together for some purpose. *We formed an organization to raise money for a new park.*

Talk about different clubs, teams, and other groups that are available to students at your school. Ask students to help you list them. Then say: *All of these are organizations. They are groups formed for a certain purpose.* Ask: *What is the purpose for each of these organizations?* Then have students complete the Day 4 activities on page 16. You may want to do the first one as a group.

DAY 5

Have students complete page 17. Call on students to read aloud their answers to the writing activity.

Day 1 organize • organization

1. How would you complete these sentences? Say them aloud to a partner.

One thing I need to better organize is _____.

The organization of books on a shelf could be by _____.

2. After you *organize* something, which words describe the results? Circle your answers.

    a. neat   c. confusing

    b. messy   d. in order

3. Which phrase describes a way of *organization* for food items? Circle your answer.

    a. many fruits and vegetables

    b. cans on one shelf and boxes on another

    c. healthy, low-fat snacks

    d. no labels

Day 2 organize

1. How would you complete this sentence? Say it aloud to a partner.

I would like to help organize _____.

2. If you had to *organize* a surprise birthday party for a friend, which of the following things might you do? Circle your answers.

    a. Make a list of people to invite to the party.

    b. Do nothing except show up at the party.

    c. Blow out the candles on the birthday cake.

    d. Gather the decorations.

3. Which event would you need to carefully *organize*? Circle your answer.

    a. making toast   c. watching television

    b. having a picnic with six friends   d. riding the bus to school

4. How do you *organize* your clothes?

_____

_____

_____

Day 3 organize

1. How would you complete this sentence? Say it aloud to a partner.

Our class is sometimes organized into _____.

2. Which group could be *organized* by a school? Circle your answer.

    a. the science club   c. the city council

    b. the police department   d. the Air Force

3. Which of the following might be a reason to *organize* a group? Circle your answers.

    a. You would like to meet with other people who enjoy reading mystery stories.

    b. You would like to sleep in later in the morning.

    c. You would like to buy new clothes.

    d. You would like to start a new team in the soccer league.

Day 4 organization

1. How would you complete this sentence? Say it aloud to a partner.

My favorite organization is _____ because _____.

2. Which sentence describes a neighborhood *organization*? Circle your answer.

    a. There is only one member.

    b. The members live in different cities around the country.

    c. The members are people from the neighborhood who have a common interest.

    d. The members are all the pets in the neighborhood.

3. Which of the following is <u>not</u> an *organization*? Circle your answer.

    a. a singing group   c. your teacher and your aunt

    b. a baseball team   d. a ski club

4. Which *organizations* would you like to join? Why?

_____

_____

_____

Daily Academic Vocabulary

Day 5 **organize • organization**

Fill in the bubble next to the correct answer.

1. Which common saying describes a good method of *organization*?

Ⓐ "An apple a day keeps the doctor away."

Ⓑ "There's a place for everything and everything in its place."

Ⓒ "A friend in need is a friend indeed."

Ⓓ "Look before you leap."

2. Which things might help you *organize* your school papers?

Ⓕ paper clips, labels, notebooks

Ⓖ scissors, eraser, ruler

Ⓗ tape, markers, pencils

Ⓙ dictionary, crayons, journal

3. Which event probably would <u>not</u> require people to *organize* it?

Ⓐ a school play

Ⓑ a class party

Ⓒ a musical concert

Ⓓ a phone call from a friend

4. Which group of people would be most likely to form an *organization*?

Ⓕ ten people on the bus who don't know each other

Ⓖ twelve athletes interested in playing basketball

Ⓗ eight students who are in different grades at different schools

Ⓙ six people standing in line at the store

Writing   Describe how you *organize* your room at home. Be sure to use the word *organize* in your writing.

_____

_____

_____

_____

WEEK 3

rare • frequent • frequently
infrequent • frequency

Use the reproducible definitions on page 162 and the suggestions on page 6 to introduce the words for each day.

DAY 1

rare
(adj.) Not often seen, found, or happening. *The scientist searched her whole life for the rare plant.*

Choose a weather condition that is extremely unlikely to happen on this day in your area. Ask: *Do you think it will ___ today?* Say: *This would be a rare weather event. It is not likely to happen.* Ask: *Can you think of a rare animal?* (e.g., lemur; panda; penguin) *What else can be rare?* Then have students complete the Day 1 activities on page 19. You may want to do the first one as a group.

DAY 2

frequent
(adj.) Happening often. *His frequent smiles brighten everyone's day.*

frequently
(adv.) Many times; often. *I frequently bring an extra juice drink in my lunch.*

Say: *Name something that you see or hear often, such as trees or honking horns.* After responses, say: *Yes, that is a frequent sound,* or *Yes, that is a frequent sight.* Say: *The word frequent is used to describe things that happen often. If you are describing actions, you use frequently. For example, the bell rings frequently. What other actions happen frequently?* Restate students' responses in a sentence. Have students complete the Day 2 activities on page 19. You may want to do the first one as a group.

DAY 3

infrequent
(adj.) Not happening very often. *The infrequent rainfall makes the desert very dry.*

Say: *You know what "frequent" means. The prefix "in-" means "not." Therefore, what does infrequent mean?* Have students name an experience that they have had only once or twice in their lifetimes. Turn students' ideas into a sentence using the word **infrequent**. For example, say: *I'm glad that having the flu is an infrequent experience for me.* Then ask students to form their own sentences using **infrequent**. Have students complete the Day 3 activities on page 20. You may want to do the first one as a group.

DAY 4

frequency
(noun) The number of times something happens in a given period of time. *The frequency of forest fires increases during hot weather.*

Say: *You are going to observe the frequency of noise during a 30-second period.* Then challenge students to be quiet for 30 seconds. Tell them to track the number of times they hear a sound during those 30 seconds. (Remind students how to use tally marks to keep track of occurrences.) After the time is up, ask students to give you the **frequency** of noise occurrences that they tallied. Then have students complete the Day 4 activities on page 20. You may want to do the first one as a group.

DAY 5

Have students complete page 21. Call on students to read aloud their answers to the writing activity.

Name_____

Day 1 rare

1. How would you complete this sentence? Say it aloud to a partner.

It is rare for someone our age to _____.

2. Which one is a *rare* sight to see? Circle your answer.

a. elephants in Africa

b. trees in a rainforest

c. snow in Florida

d. a dog on a leash

3. Why would a *rare* coin be more expensive than an ordinary coin? Circle your answer.

a. It is harder to find.

b. It is shiny.

c. It comes from France.

d. It is made of metal.

I'm a **rare** bird.

4. What is something *rare* that you would like to own?

_____

Day 2 frequent • frequently

1. How would you complete these sentences? Say them aloud to a partner.

I am a frequent visitor to the _____ because _____.

One thing that happens frequently in our class is _____.

2. Which of these things do you *frequently* do in math? Circle your answers.

a. add numbers

b. do multiplication problems

c. write a story

d. watch TV

3. Which drivers make *frequent* stops? Circle your answers.

a. a truck driver in a hurry to make one delivery

b. a school bus driver

c. a race car driver trying to win a race

d. a postal worker delivering mail

Day 3 infrequent

1. How would you complete this sentence? Say it aloud to a partner.

An infrequent event in the classroom is _____.

2. Which of these things is an *infrequent* event? Circle your answer.

a. a radio station playing music

b. the sun rising

c. a dog barking

d. seeing a shooting star

3. Which sentence correctly uses the word *infrequent*? Circle your answer.

a. An infrequent sound in the forest is a car horn.

b. I talk on the cellphone infrequent.

c. Every day, the teacher gave the students infrequent homework.

d. The infrequent balloon was filled with air.

Day 4 frequency

1. How would you complete this sentence? Say it aloud to a partner.

The frequency of success on tests increases when you _____.

2. Which events increase in *frequency* during the summer? Circle your answers.

a. weather reporters talking about snow and ice

b. families having picnics and barbecues

c. people visiting the beach

d. children wearing heavy jackets to school

3. Which events decrease in *frequency* during the summer? Circle your answers.

a. people going snowboarding

b. children riding school buses

c. children going to swimming pools

d. weather reporters talking about the heat

4. What would you like to have increase in *frequency*?

_____

_____

_____

Name_____

Day 5 | rare • frequent • frequently
infrequent • frequency

Fill in the bubble next to the correct answer.

1. Which sentence uses the word *rare* correctly?

   Ⓐ Don't be rare about your safety—wear your seat belt!

   Ⓑ Go to the rare of the bus.

   Ⓒ The rare book was even more costly because the author had signed it.

   Ⓓ Jeff is rare about his chances for winning.

2. Which word means the opposite of *frequent*?

   Ⓕ often

   Ⓖ regularly

   Ⓗ a lot

   Ⓙ seldom

3. Which one do you think is an *infrequent* event?

   Ⓐ a hot day in the desert

   Ⓑ ocean waves hitting the shore

   Ⓒ finding buried treasure

   Ⓓ seeing lightning during a thunderstorm

4. Which one occurs with the most *frequency*?

   Ⓕ A student teaches class.

   Ⓖ A teacher teaches class.

   Ⓗ A student assigns homework.

   Ⓙ A teacher does homework.

I'm a **frequent** flyer!

Writing   Describe an activity that you and your friends do *frequently*.
Be sure to use the word *frequently* in your description.

_____

_____

_____

_____

WEEK 4

view • argue • argument

Use the reproducible definitions on page 163 and the suggestions on page 6 to introduce the words for each day.

DAY 1

view
(noun) An opinion or idea. *Her **view** is that we shouldn't have to go to school on Fridays.*

Present a scenario and ask students to share their **views** on it. For example: *Many people are saying that kids spend too much time playing video games. What do you think about this? What is your **view**, or opinion?* Write "Our **Views**" on the board and record students' ideas. Point out that it is important to respect each person's **view**. Then have students complete the Day 1 activities on page 23. You may want to do the first one as a group.

DAY 2

view
(verb) To have a particular opinion or idea. *We **view** this problem as easy to solve.*

Select a news story or magazine article that is relevant to students. Summarize it for the students and then say: *How do you **view** this story? Do you **view** it as an important story?* Explain that when people talk about how they **view** something, it means that they have a certain idea or opinion about it. Then have students complete the Day 2 activities on page 23. You may want to do the first one as a group.

DAY 3

argue
(verb) To give reasons for or against something. *Doctors will **argue** that we should eat lots of fruits and vegetables.*

Say: *I have sometimes heard students say that homework is a bad idea. However, I would **argue** that it is a good way to learn to manage your time.* Explain that when you **argue** this point about homework, you give the reasons that form your opinion about it. Ask students to complete these sentence starters: "Some people say ___. However, I would argue that ___." Then have students complete the Day 3 activities on page 24. You may want to do the first one as a group.

DAY 4

argument
(noun) A reason given for or against something. *Their **argument** for a change in school lunches is based on giving kids healthier choices.*

On the board, write "Longer but Fewer School Days." Say: *When you argue, you give reasons to support your view. Those reasons are your **argument**. What is an **argument** for going to school more hours each day, but for fewer days in the year?* Record students' ideas. Then ask: *What is an **argument** against going to school more hours each day, but for fewer days?* Point out that all good **arguments** must include reasons. Then have students complete the Day 4 activities on page 24. You may want to do the first one as a group.

DAY 5

Have students complete page 25. Call on students to read aloud their answers to the writing activity.

Name_____

Day 1 view

1. How would you complete this sentence? Say it aloud to a partner.

My parents and I have different views about _____.

2. Which idea supports the *view* that dogs should be on leashes at all times? Circle your answer.

   a. Dogs need to run free in order to get enough exercise.
   b. Dogs do not like to be on a leash all the time.
   c. Owners should control their dogs on and off the leash.
   d. Dogs that aren't on leashes can scare people and cause accidents.

3. Match each *view* to the idea that supports it. Write the correct letter on the line.

Views	Ideas
___ Americans use too much gas.	a. All students should be on a sports team.
___ Children do not get enough exercise.	b. People should share rides to work and school.
___ Playing an instrument is an important skill.	c. People should watch less TV and spend more time talking to each other.
___ Watching too much TV is bad for people.	d. Schools should offer more music classes.

Day 2 view

1. How would you complete this sentence? Say it aloud to a partner.

I view writing as _____.

2. Which phrase best completes this sentence? Circle your answer.

As someone who loved nature, she viewed the trash on the trail _____.

   a. as a big problem   c. as not that important
   b. with joy   d. with no feeling

3. Which topics would a school principal *view* as problems? Circle your answers.

   a. students getting high test scores
   b. fights on the playground
   c. students checking out many library books
   d. large numbers of students coming late to school

Name_____

Day 3 argue

1. How would you complete this sentence? Say it aloud to a partner.

My parents think _____, but I argue that _____.

2. If you plan to *argue* for something that is important to you, what should you do? Circle your answer.

    a. Talk as loudly as possible.

    b. Keep your thoughts to yourself.

    c. Say the opposite of what you think.

    d. Have good reasons for what you think.

3. What reasons would you give if you were to *argue* for more recess? List the reasons.

    a. _____

    b. _____

    c. _____

Day 4 argument

1. How would you complete this sentence? Say it aloud to a partner.

One argument for no homework on the weekends is _____.

2. Which of the following is an *argument* against drivers using cellphones? Circle your answer.

    a. A lot of traffic accidents involve people using cellphones.

    b. We cannot stop people from making calls from their cars.

    c. Some people use cellphones while driving and are never in an accident.

    d. People should wear seat belts.

A driver should focus only on driving.

3. Which one would make you more likely to listen to someone's *argument*? Circle your answer.

    a. sentences that make no sense

    b. good reasons for what is said

    c. ideas with no reasons behind them

    d. an angry tone of voice

Name_____

Day 5 view • argue • argument

Fill in the bubble next to the correct answer.

1. Which *view* is probably held by a person who is worried about the amount of trash in our cities?

   Ⓐ Trash is not bad if you don't mind the smell.

   Ⓑ Everyone should recycle paper, bottles, and cans.

   Ⓒ People are recycling too much. They need to throw more things away.

   Ⓓ Selling more trash cans helps local stores.

2. You might *argue* that some video games are educational because they _____.

   Ⓕ can help you learn how to solve puzzles or problems

   Ⓖ are a good way to spend time on rainy days

   Ⓗ are very fast moving

   Ⓙ don't have a lot of words

3. Which sentence uses the word *argue* correctly?

   Ⓐ Her argue is that friends should never lie to each other.

   Ⓑ They will argue that more time is needed to finish the test.

   Ⓒ Our argue is over which sport is more fun to play.

   Ⓓ They argue because they agree with each other.

4. Which *argument* would a dentist make?

   Ⓕ Brushing your teeth every day is a good thing to do.

   Ⓖ Sweets and sodas will not harm teeth.

   Ⓗ Keeping your teeth clean is not very important.

   Ⓙ You should only go to a dentist if you lose all your teeth.

Writing   How do you *view* yourself as a student? Are you a fast worker, or slow but careful? Do you get good grades, or could you do better? Give at least two reasons for your *view*. Be sure to use the word *view* in your writing.

_____

_____

_____

_____

WEEK 5

outline

Use the reproducible definitions on page 164 and the suggestions on page 6 to introduce the words for each day.

DAY 1

outline
(noun) A line or shape lthat shows the outer edge of something. *You can see the outline of the lake on the map.*

Using a world map, trace with your finger the **outline** of a country. Say: *I can trace the shape of (the country) with my finger because its outline is shown by the border on the map.* Invite students to find and trace the **outlines** of other countries as you name them. Then have students complete the Day 1 activities on page 27. You may want to do the first one as a group.

DAY 2

outline
(verb) To draw the edge or shape of something. *I decided to first outline the tree before I started coloring.*

Outline something simple on the board, such as a cat, house, or cloud. As you work, ask: *Can you tell what I'm outlining here? When I make a drawing, I start by outlining the shapes and objects. How many of you draw pictures this way—outlining first and then filling in?* Invite one or two volunteers to **outline** their hands on the board. Mention that when we trace around an object or a pattern, we **outline**. Then have students complete the Day 2 activities on page 27. You may want to do the first one as a group.

DAY 3

outline
(noun) A written summary that shows the main points or ideas of something. *It is a good idea to first do an outline before you start writing a report.*

Write the basic form of an **outline** on the board. Start with "I. Things Cats Do." Ask students for examples of typical cat behavior and then fill them in below. (e.g., "A. Cats sleep during the day; B. Cats purr when you pet them; C. Cats chase mice") Explain that an **outline** is a great way to organize information. Say: *You start with a main idea or heading ("Things Cats Do") and then list below it things that either support or give an example of the main idea.* Then have students complete the Day 3 activities on page 28. You may want to do the first one as a group.

DAY 4

outline
(verb) To give the main points or ideas of something. *Please listen while I outline the plans for our field trip.*

Say: *I am going to outline the events of our day. Listen to find out what we'll be doing.* Briefly describe the main activities you have planned. Then say: *I have outlined what we'll be doing the rest of the day. I did not tell you every detail, just the main points. What are you most looking forward to?* Then have students complete the Day 4 activities on page 28. You may want to do the first one as a group.

DAY 5

Have students complete page 29. Call on students to read aloud their answers to the writing activity.

Day 1 outline

1. **How would you complete this sentence? Say it aloud to a partner.**

    Even when it's dark in my room, I can see the outline of _____.

2. **Which things have *outlines* that you can see? Circle your answers.**

    a. air
    b. maps
    c. footprints
    d. steam

3. **Which one is an example of an *outline*? Circle your answer.**

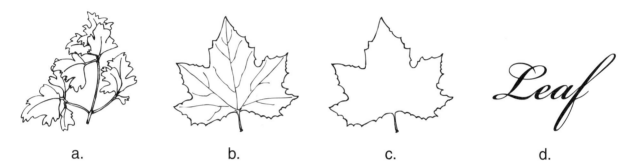

    a.   b.   c.   d.

Day 2 outline

1. **How would you complete this sentence? Say it aloud to a partner.**

    I can outline a(n) _____ by tracing it on paper.

2. **If you were to *outline* Mexico by drawing its shape, which of the following must you show? Circle your answer.**

    a. the borders and coasts of Mexico
    b. the names of all the state capitals
    c. the biggest city in each state
    d. the mountains and deserts within Mexico

3. **Which one would <u>not</u> be part of the process of *outlining* an object? Circle your answer.**

    a. looking at the object
    b. drawing its edges to show its shape
    c. tracing the object if it is flat
    d. showing all the details of what it looks like

Daily Academic Vocabulary

Day 3 | outline

1. **How would you complete this sentence? Say it aloud to a partner.**

   An outline on the topic "My Best Friend" would include these main ideas: _____.

2. **Which of these would not be included in an *outline* you made while reading a science article? Circle your answer.**

   a. main ideas
   b. key details
   c. names of characters
   d. important facts

3. **Why is an *outline* a useful way to present information? Circle your answers.**

   a. It helps you to see main ideas and details quickly.
   b. It lists every detail so you don't forget a single word.
   c. It checks whether the information is correct.
   d. It allows you to organize your thoughts clearly.

Day 4 | outline

1. **How would you complete this sentence? Say it aloud to a partner.**

   Outlining helps us remember information we read or hear because _____.

2. **Which of these would you not do when *outlining* information for someone? Circle your answers.**

   a. include all the details
   b. organize the information
   c. give the main ideas
   d. write a story using the information

3. **List three main ideas you would include if you were *outlining* ideas for a report about your favorite hobby. First read the example.**

   My Favorite Hobby: Reading Books

     I. Types of Books That I Like to Read
    II. Books That I Have Recently Read
   III. My Favorite Books of All Time

   My Favorite Hobby: _____

     I. _____

    II. _____

   III. _____

Name_____

Fill in the bubble next to the correct answer.

1. Which two animals would have *outlines* that look similar?

Ⓐ a bat and a snake

Ⓑ a tiger and an elephant

Ⓒ a mouse and a rat

Ⓓ a butterfly and an ant

2. Which sentence describes a good way to *outline* a leaf?

Ⓔ Write a story about a leaf.

Ⓕ Trace around the outside of a real leaf with a pencil.

Ⓖ Color a piece of paper green.

Ⓗ Put flowers, stems, and other parts of a plant around a real leaf.

3. When you make an *outline* for a report that you will write, which one do you include?

Ⓐ the main ideas that you will include in the report

Ⓑ every fact you learned about the topic of the report

Ⓒ a list of things you will do after you finish the report

Ⓓ reasons why you think that this will be your best report

4. An *outline* of your plans to get better grades might include all of the following except _____.

Ⓔ the main steps you will take to be a better student

Ⓕ your ideas on what makes a good summer vacation

Ⓖ your ideas about what makes a student successful

Ⓗ the reason why you want to improve your grades

Writing   Describe in two sentences why you might find an *outline* useful when you write about a topic. Be sure to use the word *outline* in your answer.

_____

_____

_____

_____

Daily Academic Vocabulary

effect • affect • impact

Use the reproducible definitions on page 165 and the suggestions on page 6 to introduce the words for each day.

DAY 1

effect
(noun) Something that happens as a result of something else. *One **effect** of the hot weather is that more people are using the swimming pool.*

Have a glass of water and a straw handy. Ask: *If I put the straw into the glass and then blow into the straw, what will happen?* After students make guesses, demonstrate. Say: *The **effect** of blowing into the straw is that I make bubbles. It is what happened as a result of something else.* Point out that some events can have several **effects**. (e.g., hot weather: people stay indoors more) Then have students complete the Day 1 activities on page 31. You may want to do the first one as a group.

DAY 2

affect
(verb) To have an effect on or to change someone or something. *His illness will **affect** my plans to go to the park on Saturday.*

Point out to students that even though **affect** and "effect" can easily be confused, the words, while related, are not the same and are pronounced differently. Write the words and their parts of speech on the board. Emphasize the pronunciations of "effect" and **affect** as you say: *For example, it is known that smoking can **affect** your health. In other words, smoking can have an effect on your health. **Affect** is usually a verb, and "effect" is usually a noun. When you **affect** something, you have an effect.* Ask: *What else can **affect** your health?* After students answer, point out the effects they mentioned. Then have students complete the Day 2 activities on page 31. You may want to do the first one as group.

DAY 3

affect
(verb) To touch the feelings of someone. *Certain songs always **affect** my mood, making me feel happy or sad.*

Tell students about a kind act done by a student from a previous year. Describe how you were **affected** by this act of kindness. (Be sure to use the word **affect** instead of "touch," or another synonym.) Say: *People can **affect** our feelings by what they say and do. We **affect** other people, too, which is why we should be careful with our words and actions.* Ask: *What things **affect** you?* Then have students complete the Day 3 activities on page 32. You may want to do the first one as a group.

DAY 4

impact
(noun) The strong effect that something has on a person or thing. *The book about ants had an **impact** on how I feel about insects.*

Ask students who has made a difference in their lives. Say: *People or events that have an **impact** on our lives change, or affect, how we think, feel, or act. Who has been very important to you? Who has had an **impact** on your life?* Encourage students to use the word **impact** in their responses. Then have students complete the Day 4 activities on page 32. You may want to do the first one as a group.

DAY 5

Have students complete page 33. Call on students to read aloud their answers to the writing activity.

Daily Academic Vocabulary

Day 1 effect

1. How would you complete this sentence? Say it aloud to a partner.

Some effects of a longer school year might include _____.

2. Which of these is <u>not</u> the *effect* of a snowstorm? Circle your answer.

   a. School is closed due to icy roads.
   b. A class takes a field trip to see a weather station.
   c. The schoolyard is covered with snow.
   d. People must shovel snow out of their driveways.

3. Which one is an *effect* of having the classroom rules written on a poster? Circle your answer.

   a. The plants don't get watered.
   b. The teacher is angry with the students.
   c. Students know what is expected of them.
   d. Lunch starts at the same time every day.

Day 2 affect

1. How would you complete this sentence? Say it aloud to a partner.

When I don't get enough sleep, it affects my _____.

2. How can students *affect* how well they do in school? Circle your answers.

   a. by dressing in nice clothes   c. by doing all their homework
   b. by listening carefully in class   d. by having lots of friends

3. List two things that *affect* how much you like a book or story.

   a. _____

   b. _____

4. List two people that *affect* your life.

   a. _____

   b. _____

**Daily
Academic
Vocabulary**

Day 3 | affect

1. How would you complete this sentence? Say it aloud to a partner.

A story that affected me was _____.

2. Which events would you expect to *affect* families in strong ways? Circle your answers.

a. a wedding   c. going to the movies
b. a picnic   d. the birth of a child

3. Which sentence uses *affect* correctly? Circle your answer.

a. The mother was so affected by her baby's first smile that she cried tears of joy.
b. The cut on the dog's paw became affected so he went to the vet.
c. The damaged house was just one affect of the tornado.
d. I would affect you if you do not do what I ask.

4. List two things people can do to *affect* the feelings of others. Tell how each action might *affect* the person or make the person feel.

Example: saying something nice makes people feel happy

a. _____

b. _____

Day 4 | impact

1. How would you complete this sentence? Say it aloud to a partner.

_____ had an impact on me when I was little because _____.

2. Which one is not a possible *impact* of our school receiving money for 100 new computers? Circle your answer.

a. More students would be able to use computers.
b. Students would learn more about how computers work.
c. Fewer students would get to use computers.
d. Teachers would use the computers in their classrooms.

3. Which one best completes this sentence? Circle your answer.

The impact of humans building on land where wild animals live is _____.

a. called "Animal Land"
b. that the animals will have fewer places to live
c. a good thing for the animals
d. that a new zoo will be built

Name_____

Day 5 **effect • affect • impact**

Fill in the bubble next to the correct answer.

1. An *effect* is _____.

Ⓐ the reason why something happens

Ⓑ what happens as a result of something else

Ⓒ a happy feeling

Ⓓ an agreement between two people

2. Which word could replace *affect* in this sentence?

Reading this amazing book will affect what many people think about snakes.

Ⓕ see

Ⓖ create

Ⓗ bother

Ⓙ change

3. If a friend's actions *affect* you deeply, then he has _____.

Ⓐ made you feel strong emotions

Ⓑ put you to sleep

Ⓒ helped you with your homework

Ⓓ dug a hole in your yard

4. Which of the following might describe somebody who has had a big *impact* on your life?

Ⓕ a distant relative

Ⓖ a careless person

Ⓗ a total stranger

Ⓙ a role model

Writing What *effect* do shorter days in the winter have on your daily activities? How does this *affect* your feelings and moods? Be sure to use *affect* and *effect* in your writing.

_____

_____

_____

_____

identify • identification
identical

Use the reproducible definitions on page 166 and the suggestions on page 6 to introduce the words for each day.

DAY 1

identify
(verb) To show what or who something is. *She could not **identify** the man in her dream.*

identification
(noun) The act of showing who a person or thing is. *The **identification** of each plant was the first step in the science experiment.*

Hold up various objects, such as desk supplies. Ask: *Can you **identify** this object? What is it?* Hold up several pens or pencils. Ask: *Can you **identify** this group?* Point to a student. Ask: *Can you **identify** this student?* Then say: *When you **identified** those things, you made **identifications**.* Ask: *When are you asked to make **identifications** in school? What are you asked to **identify**?* Encourage students to use **identify** and **identification** in their responses. Then have students complete the Day 1 activities on page 35. You may want to do the first one as a group.

DAY 2

identify
(verb) To think of one thing as being connected to another thing. *I **identify** ice cream with summer.*

Write a sentence starter on the board: "I **identify** ___ with ___." Give an example of one possible pairing. Say: *I **identify** wisdom with old age. That means that when I think about wisdom, I connect it to older people.* List words below the first blank in the sentence starter (e.g., success), and have students suggest how to fill in the second blank. Then have students complete the Day 2 activities on page 35. You may want to do the first one as a group.

DAY 3

identical
(adj.) Exactly alike. *The mother and daughter sound **identical** on the phone.*

Have students take out a textbook that they all have. Say: *Your books are all **identical**. They are all alike.* See if students can find other **identical** things in the classroom. Then point out things that are similar, but not **identical**. For example, say: *These two backpacks are similar, but they are not **identical**. To be **identical**, two things have to be exactly alike.* Then have students complete the Day 3 activities on page 36. You may want to do the first one as a group.

DAY 4

identification
(noun) Something that proves who you are, such as a card with your name and picture on it. *A passport is the **identification** you need to travel to another country.*

Show a form of **identification**. Say: *This is my **identification**. It proves that I am who I say I am.* Ask: *What are other forms of **identification**? Why are forms of **identification** necessary?* Then have students complete the Day 4 activities on page 36. You may want to do the first one as a group.

DAY 5

Have students complete page 37. Call on students to read aloud their answers to the writing activity.

Name_____

Day 1 · identify • identification

1. **How would you complete these sentences? Say them aloud to a partner.**

   I can identify the main character in a story by _____.

   The identification of the cause of a problem is important because _____.

2. **Which ones would you expect a detective to *identify* in a mystery story? Circle your answers.**

   a. suspects in a crime   c. lunch

   b. car radio   d. clues

3. **Which one would <u>not</u> help with the *identification* of a historic event? Circle your answer.**

   a. knowing when it took place

   b. knowing where it took place

   c. knowing who was there

   d. knowing that it didn't happen today

Day 2 · identify

1. **How would you complete this sentence? Say it aloud to a partner.**

   I hope that people identify me with _____.

2. **Which word means the same as *identify* as it is used in this sentence? Circle your answer.**

   I identify speed with race cars.

   a. show   c. connect

   b. discuss   d. see

3. **With whom or what do you *identify* these big ideas? Write a suggestion for each one.**

Big Idea	I Identify It With
a. hard work	_____
b. kindness	_____
c. comfort	_____

Name _____

Daily Academic Vocabulary

Day 3 | identical

1. **How would you complete this sentence? Say it aloud to a partner.**

   No two stories are identical because _____.

2. **If a dog had *identical* puppies, what might you say about them? Circle your answers.**

   a. "They look different from each other."
   b. "They look exactly alike."
   c. "One is smaller and darker than the other."
   d. "I cannot tell them apart."

3. **Which set of two problems are *identical*? Circle your answer.**

   a. 54   100   b. 8   c. 46   46   d. 54   46
      +46   - 46   x6   48 ÷ 6 = 8   + 58 + 58   - 3   - 5
      ───   ────   ──   ──── ────   ───   ───
      100   54   48   104   104   51   41

Day 4 | identification

1. **How would you complete this sentence? Say it aloud to a partner.**

   A proper form of identification should include _____.

2. **Which one would probably <u>not</u> appear on a form of *identification*? Circle your answer.**

   a. your name
   b. your date of birth
   c. your address
   d. your favorite food

3. **No two sets of fingerprints are the same. Why does this fact make fingerprints a good form of *identification*? Circle your answer.**

   a. No one else's fingerprints are like yours.
   b. Your fingerprints are like your mother's.
   c. Not everyone has his or her fingerprints taken.
   d. Animals have paw prints, not fingerprints.

Here is my identification.

Day 5 | identify • identification • identical

Fill in the bubble next to the correct answer.

1. Which meaning of *identify* would <u>not</u> fit in this sentence?

The woman could not identify the man who stole her purse.

Ⓐ recognize

Ⓑ connect

Ⓒ name

Ⓓ spot

2. Which one could help with the *identification* of a flower you have never seen before?

Ⓕ a nature book with pictures of different flowers

Ⓖ a cookbook with pictures of foods from Italy

Ⓗ a picture book of animals

Ⓙ a Spanish-English dictionary

3. For which thing would you <u>not</u> be able to find an *identical* match?

Ⓐ blue socks sold at the mall

Ⓑ a new science textbook

Ⓒ a new toothbrush

Ⓓ your home phone number

4. Which of these is <u>not</u> a form of *identification*?

Ⓕ fingerprints

Ⓖ a library card

Ⓗ a typed letter

Ⓙ a driver's license

Writing Write a description of someone with whom you *identify*. Be sure to include one sentence like this: I *identify* with _____ because _____.

_____

_____

_____

_____

select • selection • section
passage • segment

Use the reproducible definitions on page 167 and the suggestions on page 6 to introduce the words for each day.

DAY 1

select
(verb) To pick or choose from a group. *I want to **select** where we will go for our spring trip.*

Display a variety of writing tools: a pen, a pencil, a marker, a piece of chalk. Say: *I **select** this (writing object) to write with.* Then write simple math problems on the board. Call on a student, saying: *I **select** you to answer the question.* Ask: *What else do you **select** during the school day?* Then have students complete the Day 1 activities on page 39. You may want to do the first one as a group.

DAY 2

selection
(noun) The act of picking out or choosing someone or something from a group. *We made our **selection** from the list of sandwiches.*

(noun) A person or thing that is chosen. *My **selection** for "best summer book" was Gertrude Goes to the City.*

Say: *When you go to the library to get a book, you have to make a **selection** from all the books in the library. You have to choose one.* Discuss other times when students make **selections**. Then say: *Once you've made a **selection**, you can talk about what you have chosen. You can say, "My **selection** is…."* Have students practice this language by answering questions. For example, say: *Who is your favorite singer?* Students should answer using the sentence starter, "My **selection** for favorite singer is…." Then have students complete the Day 2 activities on page 39. You may want to do the first one as a group.

DAY 3

section
(noun) One of the parts that makes up the whole of something. *Downtown is my favorite **section** of the city.*

passage
(noun) A short section of a written work or a piece of music. *We were asked to find the **passage** that tells where the story takes place.*

Ask: *Which **section** of a playground do you like best? Which **section** is best for climbing?* As students answer, say: *Do you think that **section** is the best part of the playground?* Have students name other places and things that have **sections**. Then say: *When you talk about pieces of writing or music, the **sections** are called **passages**. So you might say, "I like that **passage** in the chapter."* Ask students to describe their favorite **passage** in the book or story you are currently reading. Then have students complete the Day 3 activities on page 40. You may want to do the first one as a group.

DAY 4

segment
(noun) One of the parts into which a whole is divided. *One orange **segment** seemed to have all the seeds.*

Say: *Some things have parts that are described as **segments**. Fruits, rockets, and trips are some of the most common things with **segments**.* Ask: *What are the **segments** of fruits, rockets, and trips?* Then ask students if they can think of other things with **segments**. (e.g., TV series; lines) Have students complete the Day 4 activities on page 40. You may want to do the first one as a group.

DAY 5

Have students complete page 41. Call on students to read aloud their answers to the writing activity.

Name_____

Day 1 | select

1. How would you complete this sentence? Say it aloud to a partner.

I often select books to read on the topic of _____.

2. Which words mean the same as *select*? Circle your answers.

 a. pick   c. match

 b. argue   d. choose

3. You are *selecting* a book to read for a report. Put these steps in order from 1 to 4 to show how to *select* the right book.

____ Look at the table of contents to see if the book has enough information.

____ Look up books about the subject.

____ Check out the book and read it.

____ Read a few pages to make sure it's not too easy and not too hard.

Day 2 | selection

1. How would you complete these sentences? Say them aloud to a partner.

My selection for favorite television show is _____.

If I were a team captain, I would make my selection of teammates based on _____.

2. When can making a *selection* be difficult? Circle your answers.

 a. when you already know what you want

 b. when you have a clear favorite among the choices

 c. when you don't really like any of the choices

 d. when there are many choices that you like

3. Which sentence uses *selection* correctly? Circle your answer.

 a. The selection to the problem uses addition.

 b. We must vote in order to selection a new captain.

 c. The selection of a new band member is based on who is the best musician.

 d. To selection the chapter, just look at the table of contents.

Name _____

Daily
Academic
Vocabulary

Day 3 | section • passage

1. How would you complete these sentences? Say them aloud to a partner.

I like to sit in the _____ section of the bus because _____.

When I choose a passage from a book to read aloud, I look for _____.

2. Which one is not a *section* of an orchestra? Circle your answer.

    a. strings: violins, violas, cellos

    b. woodwinds: flutes, clarinets, bassoons

    c. brass: trumpets, horns, trombones, tubas

    d. fruits: apples, oranges, peaches

3. In which sentence can the word *passage* replace the underlined word? Circle your answer.

    a. The last <u>line</u> of the poem rhymes with the first two lines.

    b. The <u>part</u> that describes the elephant family is my favorite.

    c. The <u>headline</u> of the article says, "Cyclist Wins Third Place."

    d. The <u>label</u> on the map points to where the tornado struck.

Day 4 | segment

1. How would you complete this sentence? Say it aloud to a partner.

The best segment of the school day is _____.

2. Which fruit does not have *segments*? Circle your answer.

    a. banana   c. grapefruit

    b. orange   d. lemon

3. Which one best completes this sentence? Circle your answer.

If a long plane trip is divided into two segments, it means that _____.

    a. you fly straight through without stopping

    b. the airplane has two sections for seating

    c. the airplane only travels to two small countries

    d. you stop at some point, so the trip is made up of two shorter parts

Name_____

Fill in the bubble next to the correct answer.

1. Which phrase means the same thing as "making a *selection*"?

Ⓐ giving directions

Ⓑ solving a problem

Ⓒ choosing something

Ⓓ planning something

2. Which of these makes up one *section* of a grocery store?

Ⓕ the frozen foods aisle

Ⓖ the manager

Ⓗ the window

Ⓘ the shopping cart

3. Which of these is a *passage*?

Ⓐ a book

Ⓑ words to an entire song

Ⓒ part of a poem

Ⓓ a magazine article

4. Which of these does <u>not</u> have *segments*?

Ⓕ a lime

Ⓖ a weekly television series

Ⓗ a plane trip that stops along the way

Ⓘ a glass of milk

I know which answer to **select**!

Writing   If you were planning a party, what *selection* of music would you play? Describe how you would *select* the music, and name some specific songs your final *selection* would include. Use the words *select* and *selection* in your description.

_____

_____

_____

CUMULATIVE REVIEW
WORDS FROM WEEKS 1–8

affect
argue
argument
compose
composition
effect
frequency
frequent
frequently
identical
identification
identify
impact
infrequent
organization
organize
outline
passage
rare
section
segment
select
selection
view

Days 1–4

Each day's activity is a cloze paragraph that students complete with words or forms of words that they have learned in weeks 1–8. Before students begin, pronounce each word in the box on the student page, have students repeat each word, and then review each word's meaning(s). **Other ways to review the words:**

- Start a sentence containing one of the words and have students finish the sentence orally. For example:

  *A weekend activity I **frequently** take part in is…*
  *One **effect** of not getting enough sleep is…*

- Provide students with a definition and ask them to supply the word that fits it.

- Ask questions that require students to know the meaning of each word. For example:

  *How would you describe two things that are **identical**?*
  *If someone shares her **view** on a topic, what is she doing?*

- Have students use each word in a sentence.

Day 5

Start by reviewing the words in the crossword puzzle activity for Day 5. Write the words on the board and have students repeat them after you. Provide a sentence for one of the words. Ask students to think of their own sentence and share it with a partner. Call on several students to share their sentences. Follow the same procedure for the remaining words. Then have students complete the crossword activity.

Extension Ideas

Use any of the following activities to help integrate the vocabulary words into other content areas:

- Ask students to **select** an **organization** at your school or in the community, find out more about it, and then create a chart to show how it is **organized**.

- Have students **identify** the **view** expressed in a letter printed in the opinion **section** of your local newspaper. Ask students to **argue** for or against the view that is being presented.

- Have students create posters that show how humans can positively or negatively **affect** the ability of rare plants or animals to survive.

- Have groups of students **select passages** from a novel to dramatize. Have the groups perform for the class.

Daily Academic Vocabulary • EMC 2760 • © Evan-Moor Corp.

Daily
Academic
Vocabulary

| affected | frequency | identical | organization | segment |
| argument | frequently | identified | rare | selection |

Day 1

Fill in the blanks with words from the word box.

I watched a really interesting show last night. It was the first _____

in a television series about uncommon animals in Australia. The first animal

_____ was a wombat. It is unusual to see a wombat in the wild

because they are very _____. A wombat looks like a cross between

a bear and a guinea pig. It also has a pouch like a kangaroo. For six months after they

are born, baby wombats stay in this pouch, so females are _____

carrying young. I was really _____ by the story of this amazing animal.

I'm going to learn as much as I can about wombats!

Day 2

Fill in the blanks with words from the word box.

Rick hesitated. An _____ usually followed the card trick he was

about to do. People always thought he cheated somehow, but all he used was basic

math! He laid the cards down. The order and _____ of the cards

was critical. Rick named a specific card then made his first _____.

The card he picked up was _____ to the one he named! During the

next two minutes, the _____ with which he picked up the correct

card was hard to believe. He didn't get one wrong! The onlookers were too shocked

to argue.

Daily Academic Vocabulary

argue	composition	infrequent	outline	selected
compose	effect	organize	passage	views

Day 3

Fill in the blanks with words from the word box.

Rita rushed into school. The hallways were unusually quiet. It was _____ that she was this early. Today was the day, though. The winner of the essay contest was going to be announced. The chosen _____ would be printed in the school paper. The author would read a _____ from his or her work at the next school assembly. Rita was excited. Class finally started, and the principal's voice came over the loudspeaker. The _____ of his announcement was immediate. Rita's classmates started applauding. Her essay had been _____!

Day 4

Fill in the blanks with words from the word box.

Do you often have strong opinions about things? Do you like to share these _____ with others? If so, you should join your school's debate team! You get to compete against other teams and _____ for or against a topic. A debate team teaches you how to explain and support your opinions. You learn how to sort and _____ your ideas. Listing the main points of your argument in an _____ is one way. You can also work with your teammates to _____ good reasons for your argument. On a debate team, you'll definitely make others think twice!

Name_____

Day 5

Crossword Challenge

For each clue, write one of the words from the word box to complete the puzzle.

affect
argue
compose
frequent
identical
identification
identify
impact
outline
rare
section
view

Down

1. to touch someone's feelings
2. to give reasons for or against something
3. act of showing what something is
6. a strong effect
7. exactly alike
8. to show who someone is
10. not often seen

Across

4. happening often
5. to draw the edge of something
9. one part making up a whole
11. one person's ___, or opinion
12. to write

WEEK 10

detect • detectable
discover • discovery

Use the reproducible definitions on page 168 and the suggestions on page 6 to introduce the words for each day.

DAY 1

detect
(verb) To discover or notice. *I could **detect** the odor of perfume in the empty room.*

detectable
(adj.) Able to be detected; noticeable. *The officer reported no **detectable** tire tracks on the road.*

Ask students to sit quietly with their eyes closed for 30 seconds. Say: I *want you to use all of your senses except sight to **detect** things in the classroom. What can you sense as you sit quietly?* When students open their eyes, have them list the things they **detected**. Say: *We are listing all the things that were **detectable** to you. These are the things you could sense when your eyes were closed. When your eyes are open, you also **detect** things using your sense of sight.* Then have students complete the Day 1 activities on page 47. You may want to do the first one as a group.

DAY 2

discover
(verb) To find or see something before anyone else. *In my favorite dream, I **discover** a new island.*

(verb) To find out about something. *At the fair, I **discovered** how much I liked some new foods.*

Discuss the ocean and outer space as places people continue to explore. Say: *Imagine how exciting it would be for a scientist to **discover** a new type of sea creature or a new planet! How would it feel to be the first person to see something like this?* Say: *People can constantly **discover** new things about themselves and the world around them. What is something you have recently **discovered**?* Then have students complete the Day 2 activities on page 47. You may want to do the first one as a group.

DAY 3

discovery
(noun) The act of seeing or finding out something for the first time. *We all look forward to the **discovery** of cures for the world's many diseases.*

Say: *Some people say the **discovery** of fire is the most important discovery of all. The discovery of new fossils has taught us a lot about nature. The discovery of new medicines has helped save lives.* Have students list other important acts of **discovery** using the sentence starter, "The **discovery** of ___ is important because ___." Then have students complete the Day 3 activities on page 48. You may want to do the first one as a group.

DAY 4

discovery
(noun) Something that is seen or found out for the first time. *Gold was an important **discovery** in California in the 1800s.*

Explain that **discovery** can also be used to name the thing that is discovered, rather than the act of discovering it. Say: *In the sample sentence, gold was the **discovery**. Other **discoveries** in the past have been dinosaur fossils and new types of animals in unexplored forests. What are other **discoveries**?* Then have students complete the Day 4 activities on page 48. You may want to do the first one as a group.

DAY 5

Have students complete page 49. Call on students to read aloud their answers to the writing activity.

Name_____

Day 1 detect • detectable

1. How would you complete these sentences? Say them aloud to a partner.

If I get down on the ground and look very closely, I can detect _____.

In my home, some sounds are always detectable, such as _____.

2. Which things would you be likely to *detect* on a hike through a forest? Circle your answers.

   a. the sounds of farm animals

   b. many different types of trees

   c. what causes rain

   d. animal homes, such as nests or burrows in the ground

3. If something is <u>not</u> easily *detectable,* what does that mean? Circle your answer.

   a. It does not see you.

   b. You can find it without much trouble.

   c. It has a strong odor.

   d. It is not easy to sense in any way.

The fingerprints are not **detectable.**

Day 2 discover

1. How would you complete these sentences? Say them aloud to a partner.

I wish someone would discover a new _____.

It would be great to discover that I _____.

2. If someone *discovers* a place, what is true about that place? Circle your answers.

   a. There is no record in history of anyone being there before.

   b. It is a beautiful spot where many people live.

   c. The place has been a secret from the rest of the world.

   d. It is not a good place for people to live.

3. What is something that you might *discover* about old friends that you never knew before? Circle your answer.

   a. the color of their eyes   c. new talents they have

   b. their address   d. what grade they are in at school

Day 3 discovery

1. How would you complete this sentence? Say it aloud to a partner.

The discovery of _____ was important because _____.

2. Which of these words means the same thing as *discovery*? Circle your answer.

    a. reading something over again

    b. looking at something

    c. sailing to a distant land

    d. seeing something for the first time

3. Which phrase would <u>not</u> be a good choice to complete this sentence? Circle your answer.

An important event in medicine would be the discovery of _____.

    a. what causes a disease

    b. how to prevent people from getting a disease

    c. what can cure an illness

    d. how to become a doctor

Day 4 discovery

1. How would you complete this sentence? Say it aloud to a partner.

I think that one of the most important discoveries of all time was _____.

2. Which of these events could be called a *discovery*? Circle your answer.

    a. The kicker knew just how her foot should hit the ball.

    b. The man was thrilled every time he saw the mountain.

    c. The scientist used the telescope to find a meteor that no one had seen before.

    d. The people looking out to sea knew there had to be land somewhere.

3. Match each *discovery* to the person who made it. Write the correct letter on the line.

___ gold in a cave   a. police officer

___ a new cure for a disease   b. explorer

___ new clues to solve a crime   c. miner

___ an unknown island   d. scientist

Name_____

Day 5 detect • detectable • discover • discovery

Fill in the bubble next to the correct answer.

1. Which of these things should you be able to *detect*?

Ⓐ someone's thoughts

Ⓑ what your dad packed in your lunch

Ⓒ what the weather will be like next winter

Ⓓ who will win the soccer game next week

2. Which sentence uses the word *detectable* correctly?

Ⓕ The sound of laughter is detectable when no one is around.

Ⓖ The police officer could detectable the clues at the crime scene.

Ⓗ Her detectable thoughts made me laugh.

Ⓙ The smell of the sea grew more detectable as we neared the beach.

3. Which word means the same as *discover*?

Ⓐ find

Ⓑ say

Ⓒ point

Ⓓ meet

4. Why was *Discovery* a good name for an explorer's ship?

Ⓕ because explorers were not interested in going to new places

Ⓖ because explorers were good at naming things

Ⓗ because explorers were looking for places that humans had not seen before

Ⓙ because explorers had to learn many things before they sailed

Writing   It's always good to *discover* something new about the world or yourself. Write about a time when you *discovered* something interesting. Use two of the week's words as you describe the event.

_____

_____

_____

_____

responsible • responsibility

Use the reproducible definitions on page 169 and the suggestions on page 6 to introduce the words for each day.

DAY 1

responsible
(adj.) Expected to do certain jobs or duties. *We are responsible for turning our homework in on time.*

Ask: *As students, what are you responsible for doing?* List students' ideas on the board. Using the list, have students complete this sentence: "As a student, I am responsible for ___." Then ask volunteers to name chores they are responsible for at home. Say: *When you are responsible for something, you are expected to carry out certain jobs or duties.* Then have students complete the Day 1 activities on page 51. You may want to do the first one as a group.

DAY 2

responsibility
(noun) A job or duty. *Taking care of a pet is a big responsibility.*

Refer to the sample sentence. Say: *Let's say you are responsible for taking care of your pet dog. We'll assume that an adult would buy the dog's food. The adult's responsibility would then be to make sure that there was always dog food in the home. What would be your responsibilities?* List students' answers on the board under the label "**Responsibilities**." Using the list, have students complete this sentence: "One responsibility in taking care of a dog is to ___." Then have students complete the Day 2 activities on page 51. You may want to do the first one as a group.

DAY 3

responsible
(adj.) Being the cause of something. *The storm was responsible for our power going out.*

Do a quick review of cause and effect using a graphic organizer: Cause → Effect. Say: *If a storm causes power to go out, we can say that the storm is responsible for the power outage.* Using the graphic organizer, write "storm" under "Cause," "responsible for" under the arrow, and "power out" under "Effect." Ask students to give other examples using this terminology. Then have students complete the Day 3 activities on page 52. You may want to do the first one as a group.

DAY 4

responsible
(adj.) Able to do things in a dependable and trustworthy way. *I think she will be a very responsible class president.*

Say: *Think about someone you know and trust and that you can always count on. We would call this type of person a responsible person.* Ask students to list qualities that a responsible person would have. Then have students complete the Day 4 activities on page 52. You may want to do the first one as a group.

DAY 5

Have students complete page 53. Call on students to read aloud their answers to the writing activity.

Day 1 responsible

1. How would you complete this sentence? Say it aloud to a partner.

At home, I am responsible for _____.

2. If you are *responsible* for doing a task each morning, which of these statements is true? Circle your answer.

a. You are expected to do this task every morning.

b. It's nice if you remember to do the task.

c. It is someone else's duty to do the task.

d. You get a brother or sister to do the task.

3. What is a police officer *responsible* for doing? Circle your answers.

a. putting out fires

b. seeing that people follow laws

c. keeping order in the community

d. committing crimes

4. What would you like to be *responsible* for?

_____

Day 2 responsibility

1. How would you complete this sentence? Say it aloud to a partner.

My biggest responsibility at school right now is _____.

2. Which of these is <u>not</u> a *responsibility* of any good student? Circle your answer.

a. Get to school on time.

b. Follow the class rules.

c. Do what the teacher asks you to do.

d. Be very hungry at lunchtime.

3. Which of these are *responsibilities* that you would expect a good baby sitter to have? Circle your answers.

a. make sure that the baby is fed

b. train the baby to do tricks

c. keep the baby safe and out of danger

d. spend as little time with the baby as possible

My **responsibility** is to build a nest.

Day 3 | responsible

1. How would you complete this sentence? Say it aloud to a partner.

Snow can be responsible for _____.

2. Which phrase could replace the underlined words in this sentence? Circle your answer.

The great teaching of Ms. Mori is <u>responsible for</u> our improved grades.

a. the job of   c. the cause of

b. the effect of   d. what should happen because of

3. What does it mean to be _responsible_ for something that has happened? Circle your answer.

a. Your actions caused it.

b. You had no part in it.

c. You are a good listener.

d. Your actions were very polite.

Day 4 | responsible

1. How would you complete this sentence? Say it aloud to a partner.

The most responsible person I know is _____ because he or she always _____.

2. Which of these people would you say is <u>not</u> a _responsible_ person? Circle your answer.

a. a criminal

b. a firefighter

c. a letter carrier

d. a judge

3. Which of these best describes a _responsible_ person? Circle your answer.

a. is never on time, is fair

b. works hard, tells lies

c. can be trusted, does the right thing

d. keeps promises, does not try very hard

You can always count on me!

Daily
Academic
Vocabulary

Day 5 responsible • responsibility

Fill in the bubble next to the correct answer.

1. What is the most important thing a nurse is *responsible* for doing?

　Ⓐ caring for sick people

　Ⓑ wearing a white uniform

　Ⓒ acting in a calm way

　Ⓓ making patients laugh

2. Which word means the same as *responsibility*?

　Ⓕ friendship

　Ⓖ working

　Ⓗ duty

　Ⓙ hobby

3. Which of these events might be *responsible* for a forest fire?

　Ⓐ a park ranger checking on a campground

　Ⓑ a sudden snowstorm

　Ⓒ bears or other large forest animals visiting a campsite

　Ⓓ campers not being careful with their campfires

4. Which of these behaviors would you <u>not</u> expect from a *responsible* student?

　Ⓕ studying for tests

　Ⓖ turning in homework late

　Ⓗ joining class discussions

　Ⓙ following school rules

Writing　Choose one of these areas of *responsibility,* and write at least two sentences about how a person should act to meet that *responsibility.* Use one of this week's words in your description.

baby sitter • pet owner • teacher

_____

_____

_____

experience • background

Use the reproducible definitions on page 170 and the suggestions on page 6 to introduce the words for each day.

DAY 1

experience
(noun) Something that a person has done or lived through. *Summer camp was an amazing experience that I will never forget.*

(verb) To live through or undergo. *Everyone should experience the thrill of downhill skiing.*

Ask: *What experience have you had that you never want to forget? Think about what you did, and remember what made the experience so special.* Write students' responses on the board. Then say: *An experience is something that you have done. But you can also use the word experience as a verb meaning "to do something." You can say, for example, "I will experience my first plane trip when we go to see my uncle."* Call on several students to complete the sentence "I would like to experience...." Then have students complete the Day 1 activities on page 55. You may want to do the first one as a group.

DAY 2

experience
(noun) The knowledge or skill gained by doing something. *Our newest player has lots of experience playing goalie.*

Read aloud a short want ad that asks for experience of some sort. Say: *To get most jobs, you need experience in doing certain things. That means you need specific types of knowledge or skills. Often employers look for the experience that comes from working in a job over time.* Ask students to name hobbies, sports, or artistic endeavors that they have experience with. Then have students complete the Day 2 activities on page 55. You may want to do the first one as a group.

DAY 3

background
(noun) The part of a picture or scene that is behind the main subject. *I decided to use yellow to color the background of my picture.*

Refer to a large image displayed in your classroom, such as a poster. Point to the background and say: *This is the background. It is behind the main part of the picture.* Have volunteers look out the window and describe the background against which a large foreground object is positioned. Then have students complete the Day 3 activities on page 56. You may want to do the first one as a group.

DAY 4

background
(noun) The events and conditions that lead up to or help explain another event or situation. *The information that the TV reporter gave provided background to help viewers understand why the factory closed.*

Explain to students that understanding ideas often requires that you already know some information. For example, students had to know about adding and subtracting numbers before learning to multiply and divide them. They needed the background of their earlier math lessons. Ask students to suggest examples of background they would need to complete social studies, science, and language arts lessons. Then have students complete the Day 4 activities on page 56. You may want to do the first one as a group.

DAY 5

Have students complete page 57. Call on students to read aloud their answers to the writing activity.

Name_____

Day 1 · experience

1. **How would you complete these sentences? Say them aloud to a partner.**

   The most amazing experience I ever had at school was _____.

   Sometime in my life I hope to experience _____.

2. **Which of these is an *experience* that only an astronaut might have? Circle your answer.**

   a. studying science and math in college

   b. learning about the stars and planets

   c. seeing Earth from outer space

   d. flying for the first time

3. **If someone has *experienced* the sights, sounds, and tastes of many different countries, what would you guess about that person? Circle your answer.**

   a. The person has traveled a lot.

   b. The person likes many different types of music.

   c. The person watches too much television.

   d. The person eats out often.

Day 2 · experience

1. **How would you complete this sentence? Say it aloud to a partner.**

   An activity I have lots of experience with is _____.

2. **Which jobs most likely require *experience* with children? Circle your answers.**

   a. baker

   b. preschool teacher

   c. guide for school groups at a zoo

   d. motorcycle repair worker

3. **Which set of skills should improve as you gain *experience* as a student? Circle your answer.**

   a. fishing, hunting

   b. cooking, cleaning

   c. planting, raking

   d. reading, writing

4. **What job would you like to have as an adult? What *experience* will you need for that job?**

   _____

   _____

Day 3 | background

1. **How would you complete this sentence? Say it aloud to a partner.**

    For a play about a prince and princess, the stage should have
    a background of _____.

2. **Which of the following would most likely appear in the *background* of a class photo? Circle your answer.**

    a. the class

    b. the teacher

    c. a curtain or screen

    d. a sign held by one of the students that tells what class it is

3. **Four different posters hang on a wall. Match the subject of each poster to what might appear in the *background* of the poster.**

Main Subject of the Poster	Background
___ child throwing trash on the ground	a. blue sky with few clouds
___ someone skiing down a mountain	b. a garden of flowers
___ a packet of seeds	c. a city street full of litter
___ a plane taking off	d. snow-covered trees

Day 4 | background

1. **How would you complete this sentence? Say it aloud to a partner.**

    Before traveling to a different country, it would be helpful to learn
    the background about _____.

2. **Chen's class is learning about the solar system. Which of these would be good *background* for those lessons? Circle your answers.**

    a. how the planets got their names

    b. the multiplication table

    c. some facts about the sun

    d. how to make a mobile

3. **Which of these is <u>not</u> a good resource for finding out *background* on a science topic? Circle your answer.**

    a. an art supply store

    b. the Internet

    c. a public library

    d. an encyclopedia

Daily Academic Vocabulary

Day 5 experience • background

Fill in the bubble next to the correct answer.

1. Which phrase describes an *experience* every pilot has had?

Ⓐ flying a plane

Ⓑ going faster than the speed of sound

Ⓒ visiting a foreign country

Ⓓ becoming a hero

2. Jamal says he wants to *experience* a hot-air balloon ride. What does he want to do?

Ⓕ remember the times he has flown in a hot-air balloon

Ⓖ study the history of hot-air balloons

Ⓗ invent a new kind of hot-air balloon

Ⓙ take his first ride in a hot-air balloon

I have a lot of **experience** in flying.

3. A house builder wants to hire someone with *experience* in making bricks. What kind of person is she looking for?

Ⓐ a person who is eager to learn about making bricks

Ⓑ a person who has made bricks before

Ⓒ a person who loves the idea of building brick houses

Ⓓ a person who knows that bricks are good for building

4. Which sentence best describes the *background* of a picture?

Ⓕ It is at the center of the scene.

Ⓖ It is the way the artist sees the picture.

Ⓗ It is behind the main part of the picture.

Ⓙ It is how the colors blend together.

Writing Think about something you know a lot about. If you were teaching someone else about this subject, what *background* would you share with that person at the beginning? Be sure to use the word *background* in your writing.

_____

_____

_____

_____

Daily Academic Vocabulary

indicate • indication signal

Use the reproducible definitions on page 171 and the suggestions on page 6 to introduce the words for each day.

DAY 1

indicate
(verb) To point out something clearly. *Several signs along the way* **indicate** *where to turn.*

Show a road map. Say: *This map is very helpful. It* **indicates** *to me how to get someplace or how to do something. The best maps are very easy to follow. They* **indicate** *things clearly.* Ask: *What other types of things can* **indicate** *something?* (e.g., people; stoplights) *What* **indicates** *to you what to do on a test?* Then have students complete the Day 1 activities on page 59. You may want to do the first one as a group.

DAY 2

indicate
(verb) To be a sign of something. *Birds starting to sing can* **indicate** *that spring is coming.*

indication
(noun) Anything that is a sign of something. *A fever is an* **indication** *of sickness.*

Write this list on the board: "1. It is getting dark later in the day. 2. I saw flowers blooming. 3. I heard birds singing." Ask: *What do these things* **indicate**? After students answer, say: *When something seems to be a sign of something else, we use the word* **indicate**. *For example, "Itchy eyes and sneezing can* **indicate** *an allergy."* Further explain that the word **indication** is used to talk about the sign itself. Say: *For example, "Itchy eyes and sneezing are often an* **indication** *of an allergy."* Then have students complete the Day 2 activities on page 59. You may want to do the first one as a group.

DAY 3

signal
(noun) Any word or action agreed upon as a warning, message, or command. *A soft tap on the wall was our* **signal** *that someone was coming.*

Review bike safety **signals**. Stand with your back to them as you demonstrate the **signals** for them to copy. To indicate a left turn, extend the left arm straight out. For a right turn, extend the left arm with the elbow bent to create a 90° angle going up. To indicate that you are going to stop, extend the left arm with the elbow bent to create a 90° angle going down. Have students demonstrate other **signals**, such as holding the index finger to the lips for "Shh!" Then have students complete the Day 3 activities on page 60. You may want to do the first one as a group.

DAY 4

signal
(verb) To send a signal to someone or something. *Kirsten* **signaled** *me by waving her arms.*

Say: *We can* **signal** *to others in many ways.* Ask: *How do I* **signal** *for you to be quiet without using words? How do you* **signal** *that you know the answer to a question?* Then have students complete the Day 4 activities on page 60. You may want to do the first one as a group.

DAY 5

Have students complete page 61. Call on students to read aloud their answers to the writing activity.

Daily Academic Vocabulary • EMC 2760 • © Evan-Moor Corp.

Day 1 indicate

1. How would you complete this sentence? Say it aloud to a partner.

At our school, there is a _____ to indicate the office location.

2. Which one might you use to *indicate* which direction to go? Circle your answer.

    a. numbers   c. stairs

    b. arrows   d. smiling faces

3. Who is most likely to *indicate* where a class should sit during the assembly? Circle your answer.

    a. the teacher of the class

    b. the school nurse

    c. choir members

    d. a student in the class

Day 2 indicate • indication

1. How would you complete these sentences? Say them aloud to a partner.

When I am happy, I indicate it by _____.

Some things that are indications to me that a book will be fun to read are _____.

2. Which word could replace *indicate* in this sentence? Circle your answer.

Some people never indicate with their faces how they are feeling.

    a. pick   c. smile

    b. hide   d. show

3. Which of these might be an *indication* that winter will soon be here? Circle your answer.

    a. It is so hot that no one goes outside during the afternoon.

    b. It is very cold one morning.

    c. You are invited to a picnic at the beach.

    d. You have to finish a book report next week.

4. What things *indicate* that you might be getting sick?

_____

_____

_____

Daily
Academic
Vocabulary

Day 3 | signal

1. How would you complete this sentence? Say it aloud to a partner.

I sometimes make a signal with my hands when _____.

2. Which of these is a *signal* that someone wants to talk to you? Circle your answer.

    a. a telephone ringing

    b. headlights on a car

    c. a poster on the wall

    d. the school bell

3. In which situation would you probably <u>not</u> need to use a *signal*? Circle your answer.

    a. when you want to say something to the person next to you

    b. when you want to tell your dog to sit or do another trick

    c. when you have a cold and it is hard for you to talk

    d. when you are trying to give directions to somebody who can't hear you

Day 4 | signal

1. How would you complete this sentence? Say it aloud to a partner.

One way I often signal that I like something is to _____.

2. Which worker might use a sign to *signal* information as a part of his or her job? Circle your answer.

    a. a school principal

    b. a crossing guard

    c. a garbage collector

    d. a clothing store clerk

3. Which sentence uses *signals* correctly? Circle your answer.

    a. A dancer signals her arms to the beat of the music.

    b. A man smiles and waves good-bye as the train signals away.

    c. A woman standing next to a car with a flat tire signals to other cars passing by.

    d. A baby signals at everyone he sees.

Daily Academic Vocabulary

Day 5 **indicate • indication • signal**

Fill in the bubble next to the correct answer.

1. Which of these might *indicate* where something special is hidden?

Ⓐ a birthday gift

Ⓑ a treasure map

Ⓒ a jewelry box

Ⓓ a shopping mall

2. Which of these might *indicate* that a storm is coming?

Ⓕ dark clouds in the sky

Ⓖ a poem about the weather

Ⓗ a sunny, cloudless sky

Ⓙ a train whistle blowing

3. Which of these is an *indication* that you are having pizza for dinner tonight?

Ⓐ One of the foods in the freezer is frozen pizza.

Ⓑ You just saw a commercial on television for a pizza restaurant.

Ⓒ The smell of pizza is coming from the oven.

Ⓓ There are lettuce and tomatoes on the kitchen counter.

4. Which of these is an example of how an animal *signals* a warning?

Ⓕ The cat licks all of its fur until clean.

Ⓖ The bear cub sleeps by its mother.

Ⓗ The wolf growls as the hair on its back stands up.

Ⓙ The fish swims smoothly through the water.

Writing   Think of a *signal* someone sent you today. Write about the *signal,* describing how it was sent and what it meant. Use the word *signal* in your description.

_____

_____

_____

_____

assemble • assembly

Use the reproducible definitions on page 172 and the suggestions on page 6 to introduce the words for each day.

DAY 1

assemble
(verb) To bring or come together in a group. *Before each game, we **assemble** as a team for a pep talk.*

Say: *If I said, "Everyone who is wearing blue, please stand up and **assemble** in that corner over there. Everyone wearing white, please **assemble** at the back of the room,"* what would I be asking you to do? (e.g., to form into groups) Verify students' responses by saying: *Yes, I would be asking you to come together in groups. I would be **assembling** you into groups.* Ask students to describe times when they **assemble**. Then have students complete the Day 1 activities on page 63. You may want to do the first one as a group.

DAY 2

assembly
(noun) A group of people meeting together for a particular reason. *An **assembly** for the whole school will be held on Friday.*

Ask students to describe how they are divided into groups within the school. (e.g., by grade; by classroom) Then say: *These are all groups of students. When several classrooms within a grade, or even several grades, get together for a special meeting, this meeting is called an **assembly**.* Ask students to describe a recent **assembly** that they have been to. Tell them to explain the purpose of the **assembly** and tell which student groups were there. Then have students complete the Day 2 activities on page 63. You may want to do the first one as a group.

DAY 3

assemble
(verb) To put together all the parts of something. *The twins can **assemble** a kite faster than anyone else I know.*

Display a puzzle, kit, or other item that must be **assembled** to complete. Say: *This needs to be put together. I need to **assemble** the parts to complete it.* Ask students to name things they have **assembled**. Point out that the word **assemble** is sometimes used in cooking (**assemble** a taco) and art (**assemble** a collage). Then have students complete the Day 3 activities on page 64. You may want to do the first one as a group.

DAY 4

assembly
(noun) The act of putting parts together to make a whole. *The **assembly** of the bookshelves took several hours.*

Remind students that yesterday they told about things they had assembled. Ask them to tell something about the **assembly** of that item. Model by saying: *Yesterday I assembled a new chair. I thought it would be hard, but the **assembly** was actually pretty easy.* Then have students complete the Day 4 activities on page 64. You may want to do the first one as a group.

DAY 5

Have students complete page 65. Call on students to read aloud their answers to the writing activity.

Name_____

Day 1 assemble

1. How would you complete this sentence? Say it aloud to a partner.

A fun day would be for my friends and I to assemble at _____ and then _____.

2. Which activity does not require people to *assemble*? Circle your answer.

    a. singing with a chorus

    b. working together on a group project

    c. playing in a soccer game

    d. reading a book

3. For which of these events would students first *assemble* before the event took place? Circle your answers.

    a. taking a class photo

    b. writing your answer on the board in the classroom

    c. taking a nap after school

    d. going on a field trip

Day 2 assembly

1. How would you complete this sentence? Say it aloud to a partner.

Our school assemblies usually include _____.

2. What is the main purpose of any *assembly*? Circle your answer.

    a. to bring people together

    b. to separate people into groups

    c. to take a field trip somewhere

    d. to practice a fire drill

3. Which word best replaces *assemblies* in this sentence? Circle your answer.

The United Nations hosts important assemblies of world leaders.

    a. classes   c. governments

    b. meetings   d. trips

4. Describe the best *assembly* you have attended.

_____

_____

Name_____

Day 3 | assemble

1. How would you complete this sentence? Say it aloud to a partner.

I would need help to assemble a _____.

2. Which of these things had to be *assembled* by somebody? Circle your answers.

    a. a shiny rock

    b. a necklace of beads and shells

    c. a forest meadow

    d. a model airplane

3. Emilio is at the store. He wants to buy something he will <u>not</u> have to *assemble*. Which one should he choose? Circle your answer.

    a. a set of building blocks

    b. a jigsaw puzzle with 50 pieces

    c. a book about dinosaurs

    d. a "build-it-yourself" microscope

Day 4 | assembly

1. How would you complete this sentence? Say it aloud to a partner.

The assembly of toys sometimes requires that you use tools such as _____.

2. If a box has the words "*assembly* required" printed on it, what should you expect of the item inside the box? Circle your answer.

    a. You will have to put together at least some parts of the item.

    b. The item will be ready to use as soon as you take it out of the box.

    c. The item will only work when several people use it at one time.

    d. Several parts of the item will not be in the box.

3. Which of these best completes this sentence? Circle your answer.

_____ involves many hours of assembly.

    a. Writing a letter

    b. Reading a book

    c. Building a treehouse

    d. Eating a pizza

No **assembly** required here!

        Daily Academic Vocabulary • EMC 2760 • © Evan-Moor Corp.

Day 5 assemble • assembly

Fill in the bubble next to the correct answer.

1. An invitation says, "Please *assemble* at the boat dock at 6:00 p.m." What does that mean?

Ⓐ Guests will be helping to build the dock.

Ⓑ Guests should dress up to look like sailors.

Ⓒ Guests should come alone.

Ⓓ Guests should meet at the dock.

2. Which of these describes an *assembly* of people?

Ⓕ a crowded freeway

Ⓖ an audience listening to a speech

Ⓗ a busy shopping center

Ⓙ a sports fan listening to a game on the radio

3. Which sentence uses the word *assembled* correctly?

Ⓐ We assembled the train set in about an hour.

Ⓑ We assembled clowns in our funny clothes.

Ⓒ One person assembled outside the school.

Ⓓ The pole was assembled from a forest.

4. The directions say that the *assembly* of a desk could take several hours. Which of these statements is probably true?

Ⓕ There are one or two steps to follow.

Ⓖ It will take several hours for workers to deliver the desk to your house.

Ⓗ There are many pieces to put together.

Ⓙ You will probably have to paint the desk and let it dry.

Writing   A chef says he will make you your favorite meal. What are the different foods or ingredients the chef would need to *assemble?* Be sure to use the word *assemble* in your writing.

_____

_____

_____

WEEK 15

prompt • method
methodical

Use the reproducible definitions on page 173 and the suggestions on page 6 to introduce the words for each day.

DAY 1

prompt
(adj.) Quick and without delay; on time. *Dad is always **prompt** when picking us up after soccer practice.*

Discuss school rules regarding being on time. Say: *These rules are meant to help you learn. When you are **prompt** and get to school on time, you don't miss anything.* Ask students to suggest other times when being **prompt** is important. Have them use the word **prompt** in their suggestions. Then have students complete the Day 1 activities on page 67. You may want to do the first one as a group.

DAY 2

prompt
(verb) To get someone to do something. *When my room is messy, my parents **prompt** me to clean it.*

(noun) A signal or cue to do something. *The actor needed a **prompt** when he forgot his lines.*

Say: *When I suggest that you do something, I **prompt** you. For example, I might **prompt** you to open your book, take out paper, or form a line. When I **prompt** you, I am giving you a **prompt**.* Ask: *What kinds of **prompts** might you receive in school?* Then point out that we are sometimes **prompted** by something not spoken. Say: *For example, seeing a food commercial might **prompt** you to go to the kitchen for a snack.* Then have students complete the Day 2 activities on page 67. You may want to do the first one as a group.

DAY 3

method
(noun) A way in which something is done. *One **method** to help you remember a new word is to say it several times in a sentence.*

Ask students to describe things they do in the same way each day. For example, they might do things in a certain order when practicing a sport or solving a math problem. Explain that when people do things in a certain way, you can say that they follow a **method**. Ask: *What is our **method** for responding to a fire alarm? What is our **method** for greeting a visitor?* Then have students complete the Day 3 activities on page 68. You may want to do the first one as a group.

DAY 4

methodical
(adj.) Done in a careful way that follows a system or plan. *The **methodical** worker followed the directions step by step.*

Say: *When someone follows a method to do something, that person is being **methodical**. When you carefully follow a list of instructions, you are **methodical**.* Tell about a specific classroom task you do in a **methodical** manner. (e.g., taking attendance; grading tests) Ask: *What are some times when you are **methodical** at school?* (e.g., science experiments; projects; math problems) Then have students complete the Day 4 activities on page 68. You may want to do the first one as a group.

DAY 5

Have students complete page 69. Call on students to read aloud their answers to the writing activity.

Name_____

Day 1 prompt

1. How would you complete this sentence? Say it aloud to a partner.

I am always prompt for _____.

2. Which word means the opposite of *prompt?* Circle your answer.

　a.　early

　b.　timely

　c.　late

　d.　smooth

3. Which action could help you catch the morning bus in a *prompt* way? Circle your answer.

　a.　Get your school backpack ready the night before and wake up on time.

　b.　Sleep late and run to the bus stop.

　c.　Eat a big breakfast just before the bus comes.

　d.　Forget to set the alarm the night before.

4. Which phrase would you use to describe someone who is *prompt?*

　a.　always late

　b.　on time

　c.　slow and steady

　d.　quick as a flash

Day 2 prompt

1. How would you complete these sentences? Say them aloud to a partner.

Some common things that teachers prompt students to do are _____.

Sometimes I receive prompts at home about remembering to _____.

2. Television news reporters are *prompted* about when to talk and which camera to look at. What does this mean? Circle your answer.

　a.　The reporters are often in trouble for being late to work.

　b.　Other people give the reporters cues on when to talk and where to look.

　c.　The reporters cannot remember what they are supposed to do.

　d.　Being on time is hard for the reporters.

3. If your teacher gives you a writing *prompt* on a test, what does he or she give you? Circle your answer.

　a.　a test you have to complete quickly

　b.　the time to start the test

　c.　a cue to write about something specific

　d.　a homework reminder

Name_____

Day 3 method

1. **How would you complete this sentence? Say it aloud to a partner.**

   My favorite method for studying spelling words is to _____.

2. **Read these titles for science reports. Which report describes a *method*? Circle your answer.**

   a. "The Human Body"
   b. "The Best Way to Make an Electric Circuit"
   c. "Is There Life on Other Planets?"
   d. "The Most Common Rocks"

3. **In which classroom situation is it important for all students to follow a certain *method*? Circle your answer.**

   a. Students are to silently read a book of their choice for 15 minutes.
   b. Students in small groups are to think of ideas for the class play.
   c. Students are to watch a video about jungle life.
   d. Students are to work in pairs and follow written steps to do an experiment.

Day 4 methodical

1. **How would you complete this sentence? Say it aloud to a partner.**

   I work in a methodical way when I _____.

2. **Which word means the same thing as *methodical*? Circle your answer.**

   a. careful   c. busy
   b. sleep   d. fast

3. **Which of these is a *methodical* way to plan what you will do this weekend? Circle your answer.**

   a. You start thinking about it when you wake up on Saturday morning.
   b. On Thursday, you make a detailed list of things you want to do on the weekend.
   c. You can't decide what to do, so you decide to watch television all weekend.
   d. You talk to your friend on Saturday morning and ask her what she wants to do.

4. **What would you <u>not</u> expect to see when someone works in a *methodical* way? Circle your answer.**

   a. sloppy results
   b. step-by-step actions
   c. the worker checking the plan often
   d. careful attention to details

Name_____

Day 5 prompt • method • methodical

Fill in the bubble next to the correct answer.

1. If you promise a pen pal you will send a *prompt* reply, when should you write back?

Ⓐ after plenty of time has passed

Ⓑ as soon as possible after you receive his or her letter

Ⓒ whenever you feel like writing

Ⓓ after waiting for several weeks

2. What is the purpose of *prompts* on tests?

Ⓕ to get you to work faster

Ⓖ to point out the correct answers

Ⓗ to tell you what to do to answer the questions

Ⓙ to help you read better

3. Which book would you read to find out about a *method*?

Ⓐ *Six Steps to Building a Birdhouse*

Ⓑ *The History of the Olympics*

Ⓒ *The Life of George Washington*

Ⓓ *The Planet Mars*

Step 1: Gather sticks.

4. Which sentence describes the most *methodical* way of drawing a picture?

Ⓕ Pick some colors and some paper and get started.

Ⓖ Close your eyes and let your hand move across the page.

Ⓗ Work quickly without spending too much time on planning.

Ⓙ First use a dark color for the outline, and then carefully fill in the details.

Writing Describe a time when a family member did something nice for you that *prompted* you to thank him or her. Be sure to use the word *prompted* in your writing.

_____

_____

_____

_____

structure • support

Use the reproducible definitions on page 174 and the suggestions on page 6 to introduce the words for each day.

DAY 1

structure
(noun) Something that has been built, such as a building. *Nearly every large modern* **structure**, *such as a skyscraper, has steel in it.*

(noun) The way in which something is organized or put together. *The* **structure** *of our school day includes time for outside play.*

Talk about famous buildings, showing pictures if possible. Say: *Humans throughout time have built incredible* **structures**, *sometimes with only very basic tools.* Ask students to list different types of **structures**. (e.g., bridges; towers; skyscrapers) Explain that the word **structure** is also used when people talk about how something is organized: the **structure** of government, the **structure** of the school day, the **structure** of a story's plot. Ask students to describe the **structure** of the school day. Then have students complete the Day 1 activities on page 71. You may want to complete the first one as a group.

DAY 2

support
(verb) To hold something up in order to keep it from falling. *Stakes* **support** *small trees as they are growing.*

Say: *If I want to stand a pencil straight up on my desk, what could I use to* **support** *it?* Have volunteers use erasers to try to **support** the pencil. Say: *These erasers* **support** *the pencil. Without the* **support** *of the erasers, the pencil falls. The erasers hold up the pencil.* Then have students complete the Day 2 activities on page 71. You may want to complete the first one as a group.

DAY 3

support
(verb) To believe in something or someone. *My parents* **support** *the plan to build more classrooms at our school.*

(noun) The act of providing help and encouragement. *I was happy to give* **support** *to the class food drive.*

Say: *If you* **support** *a plan or decision, you show that you agree with the plan or decision. You can also* **support** *a person, like a politician, if you agree with or believe in what the person says or does.* Ask: *What is something our school does that you* **support**? *Why do you* **support** *it?* Explain that people can also give **support** by helping others. Ask: *What are some ways that people provide* **support** *to others? How do people give* **support** *to their favorite sports teams?* Then have students complete the Day 3 activities on page 72. You may want to complete the first one as a group.

DAY 4

support
(verb) To show to be true. *The test results* **support** *my claim that most of the students understand the material.*

Discuss how new ideas are often doubted. The people who originate the ideas have to **support** their new ideas with facts. Say: *When you argue your point of view, you need to have facts and reasons to* **support** *your view. How might you* **support** *a view or idea?* Have students complete the Day 4 activities on page 72. You may want to complete the first one as a group.

DAY 5

Have students complete page 73. Call on students to read aloud their answers to the writing activity.

Name_____

Day 1 **structure**

1. How would you complete these sentences? Say them aloud to a partner.

I would like to see a structure built entirely out of _____.

A good book report is structured to include _____.

2. Which of these is <u>not</u> a *structure*? Circle your answer.

   a. a tall mountain   c. a bridge across a wide river

   b. a skyscraper   d. a large monument in a park

3. Which phrase could replace the underlined words in this sentence? Circle your answer.

I did not know that the <u>structure of a poem</u> could take so much thought.

   a. building described in a poem

   b. way a poem is put together

   c. title of a poem

   d. poet's beliefs

Day 2 **support**

1. How would you complete this sentence? Say it aloud to a partner.

Something that can be used to support a fence that is falling over is _____.

2. If Object 1 *supports* Object 2, which of these statements is true? Circle your answer.

   a. Object 1 could fall down if Object 2 is taken away

   b. Object 2 could fall down if Object 1 is taken away.

   c. Object 1 and Object 2 do not touch each other.

   d. Both Object 1 and Object 2 are about to fall down.

3. Which of these can *support* you when you sit down? Circle your answer.

   a. blackboard   c. stool

   b. pants   d. pencil

This tree branch **supports** me as I land.

Daily Academic Vocabulary

Day 3 support

1. How would you complete this sentence? Say it aloud to a partner.

When we work in groups, we support each other's ideas by _____.

2. When you *support* someone and want to let the person know, what might you say? Circle your answer.

   a. I believe in you.
   b. Your ideas are strange.
   c. I am strong enough to lift you.
   d. I wish we could agree.

3. Which word could replace *support* in this sentence? Circle your answer.

Support poured in from all over the world after the big earthquake.

   a. Ideas   c. Help
   b. Harm   d. Strength

4. How do you *support* your friends?

_____

Day 4 support

1. How would you complete this sentence? Say it aloud to a partner.

I can support what I think by _____.

2. Van's teacher wants him to *support* this statement: Most of Earth's fresh water is found in glaciers and snowfields. What should Van do? Circle your answer.

   a. argue that the statement is not true
   b. find facts that help show that the statement is true
   c. explain his own ideas about the statement
   d. build a model of a glacier

3. Which fact would *support* your belief that a story you read was true? Circle your answer.

   a. None of your friends had ever read the story.
   b. The story was in a book of fairy tales.
   c. The story was about a builder.
   d. The book's title is *True Life Adventures.*

Name_____

Day 5 structure • support

Fill in the bubble next to the correct answer.

1. Which of these is best described as a large *structure*?

Ⓐ redwood tree

Ⓑ sports stadium

Ⓒ boulder

Ⓓ whale

2. If a piece of writing has no *structure*, what would a teacher probably say to the writer?

Ⓕ You have put your ideas together nicely.

Ⓖ Your headings and ideas are easy to follow.

Ⓗ You need to organize your thoughts better.

Ⓙ You must have planned carefully before writing.

3. Your mom stands some books up between two very heavy rocks. Which sentence describes what your mom did?

Ⓐ She supported the books with the rocks.

Ⓑ She supported the rocks with the books.

Ⓒ She supported her belief that all people should read.

Ⓓ She supported her friend, who was a librarian.

4. Yukio makes a statement in class, and his teacher says he needs to *support* what he has said. What does his teacher mean?

Ⓕ Yukio needs to repeat what he said.

Ⓖ Yukio needs to really believe that what he said is true.

Ⓗ Yukio needs to show that what he said is true.

Ⓙ Yukio needs to speak more loudly.

Writing   Think of a time when you had the *support* of your friends or family. Describe how they showed their *support* and how it made you feel. Be sure to use the word *support* in your description.

_____

_____

_____

source • resource
resourceful

Use the reproducible definitions on page 175 and the suggestions on page 6 to introduce the words for each day.

DAY 1

source
(noun) The place, person, or thing from which something comes. *A dictionary is a good source for information on the meaning of words.*

Display a newspaper, a map, and an orange. Say: *All of these are **sources** of something. This newspaper is a good **source** of information about what is happening in the world.* Then point to an area on the map and describe it as a **source** of something that comes from the area. (e.g., Florida is a **source** of oranges. Find the **source** of the river.) Identify the fruit as a **source** of juice. Ask students how they would find out the **source** of the clothes they are wearing, food products they eat, etc. Remind them that a **source** can be a person, place, or thing. Then have students complete the Day 1 activities on page 75. You may want to do the first one as a group.

DAY 2

resource
(noun) Someone or something that can be turned to for help or support. *The phone book is a good resource for finding somebody's phone number.*

Describe people in your school as **resources**. Say: *Our librarian is a great **resource** when you need to find a special book. Our school nurse is your **resource** when you are ill.* Ask students to name information **resources** (encyclopedia; dictionary; Internet) and school locations (library; computer lab) where **resources** can be found. Encourage them to use the word **resource** in their responses. Then have students complete the Day 2 activities on page 75. You may want to do the first one as a group.

DAY 3

resource
(noun) Something valuable to a person, place, or group of people. *One resource for meeting our energy needs is wind power.*

Discuss **resources** that have been valuable to people throughout history. (e.g., oil; water; timber; land; minerals) Explain that a natural **resource** is usually valuable because it might run out one day. Say: ***Resources** can also be whatever is useful for a purpose.* Ask: *What **resources** would you need for an art project? For a research report?* Then have students complete the Day 3 activities on page 76. You may want to do the first one as a group.

DAY 4

resourceful
(adj.) Good at knowing what to do or where to get help. *Our parents taught us to be resourceful and make our own lunches.*

Say: ***Resourceful** people are good at figuring out ways to get what they need or at getting things done.* Have students share times when they have been **resourceful**. Remind them to use the word **resourceful** when sharing. Then have students complete the Day 4 activities on page 76. You may want to do the first one as a group.

DAY 5

Have students complete page 77. Call on students to read aloud their answers to the writing activity.

Name_____

Day 1 source

1. How would you complete this sentence? Say it to a partner.

My favorite source of factual information is _____ because _____.

2. In which sentence is the word *source* used correctly? Circle your answer.

    a. I like to source my CDs by type of music.

    b. Mom says the best source for fresh fruit is the farmers' market.

    c. My stomachaches often source from spicy foods.

    d. We should source facts from fiction in the article.

3. If explorers are searching for the *source* of a river, what do they want to find? Circle your answer.

    a. where the river ends

    b. how deep the river gets

    c. how wide the river is

    d. the place where the river begins

Day 2 resource

1. How would you complete this sentence? Say it to a partner.

I think I am a good resource for others when _____.

2. Which of these could not be used as a *resource*? Circle your answer.

    a. a book   c. a desk

    b. a librarian   d. a computer

3. Which words could be used to describe a *resource*? Circle your answers.

    a. helpful   c. harmful

    b. boring   d. useful

4. For which types of writing would you most likely need to use *resources*? Circle your answers.

    a. a short story about a camping trip

    b. a report on Spain

    c. a poem about spring

    d. a group project about how magnets work

I'm a great **resource** for academic vocabulary.

Name_____

Day 3 resource

1. How would you complete this sentence? Say it to a partner.

I think the world's most precious resource is _____ because _____.

2. Which words could be used to describe Earth's *resources*? Circle your answers.

a. comfortable   c. careful

b. valuable   d. useful

3. Different places in school need different *resources*. Match each place to its *resources*. Write the letter of the answer on the line.

Place	Resource
___ cafeteria	a. balls
___ library	b. books
___ front office	c. food
___ gym	d. telephones

This is the perfect **resource** for my report on ostriches!

Day 4 resourceful

1. How would you complete this sentence? Say it to a partner.

I felt resourceful when I figured out how to _____.

2. Which word best describes a *resourceful* person? Circle your answer.

a. clever   c. clumsy

b. angry   d. beautiful

3. Which of these actions would you <u>not</u> expect a *resourceful* person to take? Circle your answer.

a. try a different plan if the first plan does not work

b. ask for help

c. give up easily

d. come up with a new idea

Daily Academic Vocabulary

Day 5 source • resource • resourceful

Fill in the bubble next to the correct answer.

1. What does this statement mean?

China is the world's greatest source of silk.

Ⓐ Silk from China is hard to find.

Ⓑ Chinese people like to wear silk.

Ⓒ Much of the silk in the world comes from China.

Ⓓ Chinese silk actually does not come from China.

2. Felicia has a toothache. Which of these is a good *resource* for her?

Ⓕ a photo of her teeth before she had a toothache

Ⓖ a dentist

Ⓗ a glass of water

Ⓙ a dictionary

3. Which statement is <u>not</u> true about Earth's *resources*?

Ⓐ Our resources will always be here.

Ⓑ We need to use our resources carefully.

Ⓒ Our resources are valuable.

Ⓓ We cannot easily replace resources once they are gone.

4. Which statement describes a *resourceful* person?

Ⓕ This person worries all the time.

Ⓖ This person likes to collect Earth's resources.

Ⓗ This person does not like to try new things.

Ⓙ This person is good at figuring out how to solve problems.

Writing   Describe how a *resourceful* person thinks and acts. Be sure to use the word *resourceful* in your description.

_____

_____

_____

_____

assemble
assembly
background
detect
detectable
discover
discovery
experience
indicate
indication
method
methodical
prompt
resource
resourceful
responsibility
responsible
signal
source
structure
support

Days 1–4

Each day's activity is a cloze paragraph that students complete with words or forms of words that they have learned in weeks 10–17. Before students begin, pronounce each word in the box on the student page, have students repeat each word, and then review each word's meaning(s). **Other ways to review the words:**

- Start a sentence containing one of the words and have students finish the sentence orally. For example:

  *An unforgettable **experience** in life would be to…*
  *A good **background** for a painting would be…*

- Provide students with a definition and ask them to supply the word that fits it.

- Ask questions that require students to know the meaning of each word. For example:

  *What **structure** in our town do you admire?*
  *How would you describe a **resourceful** person?*

- Have students use each word in a sentence.

Day 5

Start by reviewing the word not practiced on Days 1–4: **background**. Write the word on the board and have students repeat it after you. Provide a sentence for the word. Ask students to think of their own sentence and share it with a partner. Call on several students to share their sentences. Then have students complete the code-breaker activity.

Extension Ideas

Use any of the following activities to help integrate the vocabulary words into other content areas:

- When students plan a group project, require that they tell you its **structure**, **resources** they will use, who is **responsible** for each part, and **indicate** different points at which they will check in with you about their progress.

- Have students research what they would **detect** on a nature hike in your area. Ask them to design a chart of those items. Take the hike, having them use their charts to be **methodical** as they record what they **detect**.

- Have students create a diorama of an important **discovery** in your state. Encourage them to create a **background** for the diorama that **indicates** its location and importance.

- Have students write a personal narrative describing an **experience** during which they **discovered** something new about their world.

Name_____

| assembled | discovered | indicating | methodical | resourceful |
| detect | experiences | method | prompted | signals |

Day 1

Fill in the blanks with words from the word box.

Bats are amazing animals. Did you know that they can fly in complete

darkness? They use a special way of navigating. This _____

uses sound instead of sight. It is called echolocation. A bat will send out very

high-pitched sounds. These sounds are so high that a human ear can't even

_____ them. The sounds strike anything in a bat's path,

_____ objects in its way. The sounds bounce back and give

the bat a message. This _____ exactly what is in the bat's way.

Depending on the object, the bat is _____ to keep going or

change direction.

Day 2

Fill in the blanks with words from the word box.

Sylvia Earle is a marine scientist and ocean explorer. She has

_____ many new kinds of plants and animals in the ocean. She

even figured out a way to live underwater. This _____ woman lived

in a four-room lab on the ocean floor for two weeks! She _____, or

gathered, a team of women scientists who studied with her. They were careful and

_____ in recording everything they saw. Sylvia Earle has done many

exciting and unusual things. She has given speeches and written books about her

_____. She is still exploring the ocean today.

Name_____

**Daily
Academic
Vocabulary**

| assembly | discovery | resources | responsible | structures |
| detectable | indications | responsibility | source | supports |

Day 3

Fill in the blanks with words from the word box.

Things like skyscrapers and bridges astonish me. These huge _____

are so strong! My uncle says that steel is what _____ most of the weight.

Steel is made from rock that is full of iron. This iron ore is found in England, France, and a

few other countries. The U.S. is a _____ of it, too. The rock is mined and

then heated. Once a few minerals are added to it, steel is created. My uncle thinks that

steel is one of our most valuable _____. He says we should be grateful

to the people whose job and _____ it is to mine the iron.

Day 4

Fill in the blanks with words from the word box.

The class was discussing a presentation they were going to give to the entire

school at next month's _____. They were _____

for telling the story of Christopher Columbus. Mr. Johnson explained that there is

information showing that Columbus probably wasn't the first explorer to visit the

Americas. There are _____ that others arrived first. Amy's voice

was so quiet it was barely _____. She wanted to know why we

celebrate Columbus Day. Mr. Johnson smiled. He said that our class could call it a

"day of _____" and honor all explorers.

Daily
Academic
Vocabulary

Crack the Code!

Write one of the words from the word box on the lines next to each clue.

assemble	discover	method	responsibility	support
assembly	discovery	methodical	responsible	
background	experience	prompt	signal	
detect	indicate	resource	source	
detectable	indication	resourceful	structure	

1. events that help to explain another event ___ ___ ___ ___ ___ ___ ___ ___ ___ ___
                                                        1   2

2. done in a planned, careful way ___ ___ ___ ___ ___ ___ ___ ___ ___ ___
                                     3

3. anything that points out something ___ ___ ___ ___ ___ ___ ___ ___ ___ ___
                                       4   5

4. a job or duty ___ ___ ___ ___ ___ ___ ___ ___ ___ ___ ___ ___ ___ ___
                              6

5. to notice ___ ___ ___ ___ ___ ___
                7

6. to put parts together to make a whole ___ ___ ___ ___ ___ ___ ___ ___
                                      8   10

7. the opposite of late ___ ___ ___ ___ ___ ___
                        9

Now use the numbers under the letters to crack the code. Write the letters on the lines below. The words will complete this sentence.

Because of echolocation, bats can fly in the _____.

___ ___ ___ ___   of   ___ ___ ___   ___ ___ ___ ___ ___
4 8 9 1   7 3 10   6 5 2 3 7

WEEK 19

introduce • introduction introductory

Use the reproducible definitions on page 176 and the suggestions on page 6 to introduce the words for each day.

DAY 1

introduce
(verb) To begin or start.
The speaker will introduce his talk with a funny story.

Say: *I think I'll introduce this lesson with a joke. What did one math book say to the other? I have a lot of problems!* Explain that when you start, or begin, something, you can use the word **introduce** to describe the action you take. Ask students for phrases that sometimes **introduce** stories that take place in the past. (e.g., "Once upon a time..."; "There once was a...") Then have students complete the Day 1 activities on page 83. You may want to do the first one as a group.

DAY 2

introduce
(verb) To bring in something new. *In the next chapter, the author will introduce an unexpected event.*

introduction
(noun) The first time that something is experienced. *My uncle gave me my introduction to chess.*

Say: *Let's pretend we have been studying animal groups. I might introduce marsupials—animals with pouches, such as kangaroos. When something is introduced, it is a new idea.* Ask: *What are some new ideas or skills you have been introduced to this year?* Then say: *The first time a person experiences something, we say it is that person's introduction to the experience. Tell me about your introduction to this school year.* Then have students complete the Day 2 activities on page 83. You may want to do the first one as a group.

DAY 3

introduction
(noun) The opening part of a book or other written work. *The book's introduction was written by a famous scientist.*

Show students a book that has an **introduction**. Explain that many books begin with an **introduction**, or a note to readers that introduces them to the book. In the **introduction**, readers might learn about the author, background information, or why the book was written. Ask: *Do any of you have a library book in your desk? Look to see if it has an introduction.* Have students share the **introductions**, or have more examples. Then have students complete the Day 3 activities on page 84. You may want to do the first one as a group.

DAY 4

introductory
(adj.) Serving to introduce. *The principal opened the assembly with introductory remarks about school spirit.*

Have students think of a topic they are interested in. Say: *Suppose you were to give a speech to the entire school about (topic). What would you say in your introductory remarks?* Explain that **introductory** describes anything that introduces. Then have students complete the Day 4 activities on page 84. You may want to do the first one as a group.

DAY 5

Have students complete page 85. Call on students to read aloud their answers to the writing activity.

Name_____

Day 1   introduce

1. How would you complete this sentence? Say it aloud to a partner.

If I wrote an adventure story, I would introduce it with _____.

2. Which words could replace *introduced* in this sentence? Circle your answers.

The speaker introduced her talk on India with a beautiful slide show of the country.

a. opened   c. began
b. answered   d. subtracted

3. Read the sentences about a school play. What was the order of events that night? Circle your answer.

The play was a big success. The audience stood up and clapped for a full five minutes when it was over. The drama teacher had introduced the play with kind words about the kids. That was a hit with the parents, too!

a. Play is performed. → Audience stands and claps. → Drama teacher talks.
b. Drama teacher talks. → Play is performed. → Audience stands and claps.
c. Audience stands and claps. → Drama teacher talks. → Play is performed.
d. Audience stands and claps. → Play is performed. → Drama teacher talks.

Day 2   introduce • introduction

1. How would you complete these sentences? Say them aloud to a partner.

It would be fun to introduce my friends to my favorite _____.

I have enjoyed _____ ever since my first introduction to it.

2. Which word might you see on the package of something that is being *introduced* in stores? Circle your answer.

a. strange   c. same
b. new   d. friendly

3. Ali just had an *introduction* to Chinese food. What happened? Circle your answer.

a. Ali tasted Chinese food for the first time.
b. Ali met a famous Chinese chef.
c. Ali wrote a paragraph about Chinese food.
d. Ali took his friends to his favorite Chinese restaurant.

Daily
Academic
Vocabulary

Day 3 introduction

1. How would you complete this sentence? Say it aloud to a partner.

Information I might find out from a book's introduction is _____.

2. Where is the *introduction* to a book found? Circle your answer.

    a. on the back cover   c. at the end of the book

    b. at the beginning of the book   d. between chapters

3. Which of these is <u>not</u> a reason an author might include an *introduction*? Circle your answer.

    a. to give readers important background information

    b. to explain why he or she wrote the story

    c. to tell readers how the story ends

    d. to get readers excited about reading the story

4. Write a brief *introduction* to a book about your life.

_____

_____

Day 4 introductory

1. How would you complete this sentence? Say it aloud to a partner.

An introductory paragraph can help you _____.

2. If a company announces an *introductory* offer for a product, what is true about the product? Circle your answer.

    a. It is a new product, and the company is trying to make people aware of it.

    b. It is a product that people have been buying for many years.

    c. It is a very colorful label that makes you want to buy it.

    d. It would make a nice gift for a new friend.

3. What would a speaker <u>not</u> do in her *introductory* remarks? Circle your answer.

    a. greet the audience

    b. explain what she will speak about

    c. try to catch the interest of the audience

    d. say good-bye to the audience

All **introductory** remarks should include compliments to parrots.

Name_____

Day 5 introduce • introduction • introductory

Fill in the bubble next to the correct answer.

1. **Which word means the opposite of *introduced* in this sentence?**
   He introduced the show with a joke about the hot weather.

   Ⓐ began

   Ⓑ ended

   Ⓒ interrupted

   Ⓓ continued

2. **Ana's teacher will *introduce* rules about the class rabbit when it arrives. What does that mean?**

   Ⓕ The students will meet the rabbit.

   Ⓖ The teacher will begin a story about rabbits.

   Ⓗ The teacher will tell students how they should treat the rabbit.

   Ⓙ The rabbit will be sent away for breaking class rules.

3. **Which phrase best describes a person's *introduction* to something?**

   Ⓐ new experience

   Ⓑ last try

   Ⓒ old habit

   Ⓓ wishful thinking

4. **Which sentence uses the word *introductory* correctly?**

   Ⓕ We turned to the introductory to find facts about the author.

   Ⓖ The speaker ended his speech with a few introductory remarks.

   Ⓗ I will introductory my speech with a funny story.

   Ⓙ His introductory comments helped me know what to expect from the book.

Writing   Imagine that you have been asked to speak to kindergartners on their first day of school. How would you *introduce* them to your school? Write a few of your *introductory* remarks using one of this week's words.

_____

_____

_____

WEEK
20

reveal • exhibit • display

Use the reproducible definitions on page 177 and the suggestions on page 6 to introduce the words for each day.

DAY 1

reveal
(verb) To make known or tell. *I do not like it when people reveal the ending of a movie I haven't seen.*

Ask: *What are some things that have been revealed to you in class recently?* Discuss common uses of **reveal**: to **reveal** secrets, to **reveal** a new discovery, to **reveal** the facts behind a situation. Then have students complete the Day 1 activities on page 87. You may want to do the first one as a group.

DAY 2

reveal
(verb) To uncover or bring into view. *If Grandpa takes off his hat, he will reveal his bald head.*

Explain that **reveal** can also be used to describe the process of showing something that couldn't be seen before. If your room has window coverings, use them to demonstrate how opening them **reveals** the outside world. Ask: *What could you do to reveal something?* Then have students complete the Day 2 activities on page 87. You may want to do the first one as a group.

DAY 3

exhibit
(verb) To show or display something for viewing. *The art students will exhibit their best artwork in the mall.*

(verb) To show or reveal feelings, behaviors, or signs of something. *I never exhibit my anger in a hurtful way.*

Talk with students about why you like to **exhibit** their best work for Open House at your school. Say: *I like to show off your great work to your parents and other visitors, so I exhibit it on the walls. What other items does the school exhibit?* Explain that **exhibit** can also be used to describe how people act, or show their feelings, toward others. Ask: *If someone exhibits happiness, what might he or she do? How might a person exhibit fear during a scary movie?* Then have students complete the Day 3 activities on page 88. You may want to do the first one as a group.

DAY 4

display
(verb) To put on view or show something. *We proudly display our trophies in a glass case.*

(noun) Something that is put on view for everyone to see. *The museum's display of old masks is amazing.*

Explain that the verb **display** means the same thing as "exhibit." Say: *I could say that "I exhibit your artwork for Open House," or I could say that "I display it…." The meaning is the same.* Discuss **display** as a noun. Say: *When I set something up for others to look at, I have made a display. A display is something you want others to see.* Ask students to describe **displays** they have seen in museums, in stores, or around the school. Then have students complete the Day 4 activities on page 88. You may want to do the first one as a group.

DAY 5

Have students complete page 89. Call on students to read aloud their answers to the writing activity.

Daily Academic Vocabulary

Day 1 reveal

1. How would you complete this sentence? Say it aloud to a partner.

I wish someone would reveal the secret of how to _____.

2. In many countries, news reporters do not have to name the people who give them information. Which sentence below best describes this situation? Circle your answer.

   a. A news story will always reveal people's secrets.

   b. News reporters cannot be forced to reveal from whom they got their information.

   c. News reporters always reveal the names of the people to whom they talk.

   d. A good news story does not try to reveal the facts.

3. In which sentences is someone *revealing* information? Circle your answers.

   a. Juan and Gabriel discussed the movie they saw last night.

   b. Sari's teacher announced that the class would have a science test on Thursday.

   c. Bao kept the surprise ending of the story to himself.

   d. Venus told Trinity where she should look to find the bird's nest.

Day 2 reveal

1. How would you complete this sentence? Say it aloud to a partner.

It would be wonderful if one day a door would open to reveal _____ right outside our classroom!

2. Which words could be used instead of *revealed* in this sentence? Circle your answers.

She peeled off the bandage and revealed her cut.

   a. uncovered   c. showed

   b. hid   d. hurt

3. Which words best complete each sentence starter? Write the correct letter on the line.

____ The clouds disappeared to reveal   a. a stage made to look like a cave.

____ The curtain went up to reveal   b. a beautiful blue sky.

____ The twins rolled up their sleeves to reveal   c. faraway stars.

____ The scientist used a telescope to reveal   d. matching birthmarks.

Day 3 exhibit

1. How would you complete these sentences? Say them aloud to a partner.

I would like to have a collection of _____ that I could exhibit at _____.

Friends exhibit their good feelings for each other when they _____.

2. Which statement would <u>not</u> be true about a person who *exhibits* photographs? Circle your answer.

    a. The person sets up the photographs so others can see them.

    b. The person invites people to come see the photographs.

    c. The person does not want people to look at the photographs.

    d. The person describes the exhibit as a photography show.

3. If a tiger is described as *exhibiting* strange behavior, what is happening? Circle your answer.

    a. The tiger is being a good hunter.

    b. The tiger has two different-colored eyes.

    c. The tiger is watched by lots of people at a zoo every day.

    d. The tiger is acting in ways you would not expect.

Do I **exhibit** strange behavior?

Day 4 display

1. How would you complete these sentences? Say them aloud to a partner.

Our school displays _____ done by students.

If I went to a space museum, I would expect to see displays of _____.

2. Hoon wrote a fan letter to the creator of his favorite comic book. In which sentence from the letter does Hoon suggest that the artist *display* some of her drawings? Circle your answer.

    a. "Your drawings make the comic book world seem so real!"

    b. "I like being able to see what the characters are thinking."

    c. "It would be great to be able to see some of your drawings at a museum."

    d. "Someday I hope to meet you in person and have you sign a comic book for me."

3. Which description tells about a school *display*? Circle your answer.

    a. new swings on the playground

    b. trophies in a glass case in the front office

    c. books on the library shelves

    d. the national anthem playing on loudspeakers

Daily Academic Vocabulary

Day 5 **reveal • exhibit • display**

Fill in the bubble next to the correct answer.

1. Lourdes says she will *reveal* how to win the video game. What does she mean?

Ⓐ She will tell you what to do to win the game.

Ⓑ She will keep trying to figure out how to win the game.

Ⓒ She will open the box the game came in.

Ⓓ She will keep the secret to winning the game to herself.

2. Which word means the opposite of *reveal*?

Ⓕ show

Ⓖ uncover

Ⓗ exhibit

Ⓙ hide

3. Which person described below is not *exhibiting* something?

Ⓐ The museum worker tries to fix the broken piece of pottery.

Ⓑ The studio owner hangs the last painting for the big art show.

Ⓒ The florist creates a beautiful selection of roses to show at the flower show.

Ⓓ The artist checks to be sure her painting can be seen by everyone in the room.

4. Which of these things is not part of a *display*?

Ⓕ a library bulletin board with information about National Reading Month

Ⓖ a painting that is being painted by an artist

Ⓗ a store window that shows clothes sold inside the store

Ⓙ a glass case inside a museum that contains dinosaur fossils

Writing   Write about your favorite hobby. Tell whether your hobby results in something you could *display* or *exhibit*. Use *display* or *exhibit* in your writing.

_____

_____

_____

_____

WEEK 21

consult • discuss
discussion

Use the reproducible definitions on page 178 and the suggestions on page 6 to introduce the words for each day.

DAY 1

consult
(verb) To go to another person or other source for information or advice. *My parents always consult a doctor when I have a fever.*

Say: *When I need information or advice, I need to consult with an expert on the subject. I need to ask someone else for help.* Pose some scenarios and ask students to suggest whom they might **consult**. Say: *You have had a toothache for three days. Whom do you consult?* OR *You don't understand a math word problem. Whom do you consult?* OR *You don't know where a book is in the library. Whom do you consult?* Then have students complete the Day 1 activities on page 91. You may want to do the first one as a group.

DAY 2

discuss
(verb) To talk over something with other people. *We should discuss how we will present our reports.*

Explain that when people **discuss** something, everyone should take part and contribute to what is said. Ask: *If I'm the only one talking, are we discussing an idea? Tell me some situations when we have discussed things in class.* Then have students complete the Day 2 activities on page 91. You may want to do the first one as a group.

DAY 3

discussion
(noun) A serious talk about something. *I thought our discussion about the poem was very interesting.*

Have students think about the different talks they have had with people today. Explain that some talks might be described as "chats," "catching up," or other names for everyday conversations. However, a talk about something more serious can be called a **discussion**. Give the example of a **discussion** you have had recently in class. Ask students to recall class **discussions**. Then have students complete the Day 3 activities on page 92. You may want to do the first one as a group.

DAY 4

discuss
(verb) To present an idea or point of view by writing or talking about it. *The speaker will discuss his ideas for how to improve our school.*

Remind students that on Day 2 you said that to **discuss** ideas, everyone should participate. Say: *Sometimes a person might present, or discuss, his or her ideas in a group. For example, an author might discuss ideas in writing, or a speaker might say: "Today I will discuss my ideas about ___."* Then ask: *Can you remember times in class when a person discussed his or her ideas with a group?* Then have students complete the Day 4 activities on page 92. You may want to do the first one as a group.

DAY 5

Have students complete page 93. Call on students to read aloud their answers to the writing activity.

Name _____

Day 1 consult

1. **How would you complete this sentence? Say it aloud to a partner.**

   If I needed help on a math problem, I would consult _____.

2. **When you *consult* someone, what are you doing? Circle your answer.**
   a. saying mean things to the person
   b. telling the person what to do
   c. looking for help with something
   d. helping the person to feel better

3. **Why might a student *consult* a librarian? Circle your answers.**
   a. to find a great new book to read
   b. to complain about the noise in the hallways
   c. to suggest some magazines the library should get
   d. to learn how to find information about volcanoes

You can **consult** me about parrots!

Day 2 discuss

1. **How would you complete this sentence? Say it aloud to a partner.**

   My friends and I like to discuss _____.

2. **Which phrase means the same as *discuss*? Circle your answer.**
   a. make angry
   b. talk over
   c. think about
   d. say slowly

3. **Several people are *discussing* an idea. What things should each person do? Circle your answers.**
   a. listen to what others say about the idea
   b. say what he or she thinks about the idea
   c. remain silent
   d. yell at the other people

4. **You are excited about a book you just read and want to *discuss* it with others. What do you need? Circle your answer.**
   a. the author's address to write a letter about the book
   b. paper and pencil to write a report on the book
   c. a librarian to help you find other books written by the author
   d. other people to talk to who have read the book

Name_____

Day 3 discussion

1. How would you complete this sentence? Say it aloud to a partner.

My favorite class discussion this year was about _____.

2. Which of these sentences describes a *discussion*? Circle your answer.

   a. You read a report to the class about a book you just read.
   b. There is an announcement on television that there is no school today because of the snowstorm.
   c. Students and their teacher talk about healthy ways of eating.
   d. Your teacher gives the homework assignments at the end of the day.

3. Which of these is <u>not</u> needed for a *discussion*? Circle your answer.

   a. two or more people
   b. a topic to talk about
   c. everybody taking part
   d. a book to read from

4. On what topic should your class hold a *discussion*? What would you say during the *discussion*?

_____

_____

Day 4 discuss

1. How would you complete this sentence? Say it aloud to a partner.

I wish _____ would come to speak at our school and discuss _____.

2. Which words or phrases could replace *discussed* in this sentence? Circle your answers.

As part of her speech to children, the astronaut discussed what it is like to fly in space.

   a. showed slides of
   b. told about
   c. shared
   d. wrote about

3. Which sentence uses the word *discuss* correctly? Circle your answer.

   a. Some authors discuss the main ideas of their books in the opening paragraphs.
   b. I will discuss to you what I know about dinosaurs.
   c. I had a serious discuss with my friend about borrowing and losing my jacket.
   d. I did not know the sight of raw meat would discuss me so much.

Name_____

Day 5 consult • discuss • discussion

Fill in the bubble next to the correct answer.

1. **Which phrase describes the type of person with whom you might *consult*?**

   Ⓐ someone who needs your help

   Ⓑ a friend who can make you laugh

   Ⓒ a mean person who has hurt your feelings

   Ⓓ an expert in an area for which you need help

2. **Your homework assignment is: "Come to class tomorrow prepared to *discuss* Australia's geography." What should you expect to happen in class tomorrow?**

   Ⓕ You will have a social studies test.

   Ⓖ You and the other students will talk with the teacher about geography.

   Ⓗ You will quietly take notes during the geography lesson.

   Ⓙ Students will take turns reading aloud from the social studies book.

3. **Which of these is <u>not</u> true about a *discussion*?**

   Ⓐ It can be done without using words.

   Ⓑ It is a serious talk.

   Ⓒ At least two people talk and listen to each other.

   Ⓓ It is about a certain topic or idea.

4. **An author says at the beginning of a science article: "I will *discuss* the steps I followed during the experiment." What does this mean?**

   Ⓕ The article will be very short.

   Ⓖ The author will tell us in writing about the steps in the experiment.

   Ⓗ The author will tell us what he did after he finished the experiment.

   Ⓙ The author is unhappy with how the experiment turned out.

Writing   Why might someone *consult* you for help? Describe a situation when you think you might be *consulted*. Be sure to use the word *consult* in your description.

_____

_____

_____

WEEK 22

design • designed

Use the reproducible definitions on page 179 and the suggestions on page 6 to introduce the words for each day.

DAY 1

design
(verb) To draw or plan something that could be built or made. *As a final social studies project, we will **design** our own energy-saving homes.*

Talk with students about the process of constructing a building. Say: *Making a building requires a plan. Before any work begins with tools and equipment, people have spent a lot of time **designing** how the building will look. They **design** their ideas on paper. Then they often follow those plans to make a small model of the building.* Have students think of how they **design** as part of their schoolwork. Ask: *When have you had to **design** something? What did you **design**?* Then have students complete the Day 1 activities on page 95. You may want to do the first one as a group.

DAY 2

design
(noun) A drawing or plan showing how something is to be built or made. *Be sure to follow the **design** carefully when putting together the model train tracks.*

Say: *Once you design a plan for something you will make, you can then describe those results as your **design**. You might say: "Now I will follow my **design** to build the model."* Ask students when they have followed the **designs** of others to make something. (e.g., building **designs** that come with sets of blocks, such as Legos®) Then have students complete the Day 2 activities on page 95. You may want to do the first one as a group.

DAY 3

designed
(verb) To be meant for a special purpose. *The sports shirt was **designed** to keep athletes cooler.*

Take a regular pencil eraser and attempt to erase something on the board. Say: *This eraser was not **designed** to erase this board.* Then erase the board using the proper type of eraser. Say: *Now this eraser was **designed** for this type of board. It was made especially for erasing on this board.* Have students suggest objects that have been **designed** for a special purpose. Then have students complete the Day 3 activities on page 96. You may want to do the first one as a group.

DAY 4

design
(noun) A pattern made up of lines, figures, or objects. *I used brightly colored squares and circles in my **design**.*

Say: *What are some of the shapes and figures that we have studied in math?* List them on the board. Then say: *Many beautiful **designs** can be made from these. The **designs** can be made by arranging shapes and figures in a pattern.* Ask students to point out any **designs** on their clothing. Then have students complete the Day 4 activities on page 96. You may want to do the first one as a group.

DAY 5

Have students complete page 97. Call on students to read aloud their answers to the writing activity.

Name_____

Day 1 design

1. **How would you complete this sentence? Say it aloud to a partner.**

   I would like to design a _____.

2. **If you are *designing* something, what are you doing? Circle your answer.**

   a. building it
   b. trying to understand it
   c. planning it
   d. taking it apart

3. **Which of these things might a person *design*? Circle your answers.**

   a. cloud patterns in the sky
   b. a treehouse
   c. a sudden idea
   d. a model of an old fort

Day 2 design

1. **How would you complete this sentence? Say it aloud to a partner.**

   Following a design is helpful when you build a _____ or make a _____.

2. **What should a good *design* for building a kite include? Circle your answers.**

   a. steps to follow in putting together the pieces
   b. coloring book pages of kites throughout history
   c. pictures of how the kite should look
   d. information about wind and weather throughout the world

3. **Which word could replace *design* in this sentence? Circle your answer.**

   The design for my bunk bed included a list of materials to buy.

   a. tools
   b. plan
   c. guess
   d. quilt

4. **Which of these would require a well-thought-out *design*? Circle your answers.**

   a. sandwich
   b. bridge
   c. quilt
   d. tree

Name_____

Day 3 designed

1. How would you complete this sentence? Say it aloud to a partner.

Some of the objects in the classroom designed for teaching and learning are _____.

2. If a hat is *designed* especially to wear in the rain, what can you guess about it? Circle your answer.

    a. It has pretty shapes on it.

    b. It is waterproof.

    c. It has holes all over it that form a pattern.

    d. It is bright red.

3. Match each object to one group of people it is *designed* to help. Write the letter on the line.

Object	Designed to Help
___ waterproof watchs	a. jackhammer operators
___ earplugs	b. cooks
___ space helmet	c. sailors
___ food warmer	d. astronauts

Day 4 design

1. How would you complete this sentence? Say it aloud to a partner.

I really like the design on _____.

2. Which word could replace *designs* in this sentence? Circle your answer.

Native Americans used many beautiful designs in their blankets.

    a. paintings   c. clay pots

    b. rocks   d. patterns

3. Benito's teacher told him to make a *design* using geometrical shapes. What might he do to complete the assignment? Circle your answer.

    a. write a paper about how to draw circles and squares

    b. cut out squares, triangles, and circles and arrange them in a pattern

    c. trace around something rectangular and color it in

    d. use paints and a paintbrush to color in a picture of a pyramid

Name _____

Day 5 design • designed

Fill in the bubble next to the correct answer.

1. Why do people *design* things before building them?

Ⓐ to prove that they are good artists

Ⓑ to have fun picking out the right colors

Ⓒ because careful planning leads to good results

Ⓓ because they want to see what happens without planning

2. When you look at a *design* while building something, what are you doing?

Ⓕ following the instructions

Ⓖ being very creative

Ⓗ making a pattern

Ⓙ forming your own plans

3. Which phrase could replace the underlined words in this advertising message?

New fireproof clothing <u>designed for</u> firefighters is on sale!

Ⓐ illustrated by

Ⓑ made especially for

Ⓒ built by

Ⓓ named after

4. Carly's teacher gave her buttons, ribbons, shells, and beads, and told her to make a *design* with the objects. What should Carly do?

Ⓕ stack the objects on top of each other

Ⓖ place the objects in a big pile

Ⓗ use the objects in a science experiment

Ⓙ glue the objects onto something to create a pattern

Writing   Imagine that you have been asked to *design* the cover for your favorite book. Write about your ideas for the *design,* using one of this week's words.

_____

_____

_____

vary • variation
various • variety

Use the reproducible definitions on page 180 and the suggestions on page 6 to introduce the words for each day.

DAY 1

vary
(verb) To be different or become different from what was before. *The date of Thanksgiving will often vary because the holiday must be on a Thursday.*

Discuss your daily schedule with students. Ask: *When does our schedule vary? When do we do things in a different way?* Have students think of other things they could describe as **varying** or becoming different. Encourage them to use the word **vary**. Then have students complete the Day 1 activities on page 99. You may want to do the first one as a group.

DAY 2

variation
(noun) A change from the usual. *I look forward to the variation in my schedule during summer.*

Remind students of the meaning of the verb "vary." Ask: *If I say we will vary the order of our lessons today, what can you expect?* Then explain that the change itself is called a **variation**. Give an example. Say: *If we vary the order of lessons, you can expect variation in what we study first, second, and so on.* Then have students complete the Day 2 activities on page 99. You may want to do the first one as a group.

DAY 3

variation
(noun) A slightly different form or version of something. *The school cafeteria serves a different variation of pizza every day.*

Review the meaning of **variation** from Day 2. Then explain that this word has a second meaning. Quickly draw on the board several different sketches of a simple object, such as the sun, a flower, or a stick figure. Say: *These sketches are all of a (name the object), but each one is slightly different. They are all variations of a (name the object).* Discuss some common usages of **variation**. (e.g., when describing art, music, ideas, or ways of serving a food) Ask students for examples in each category. Then have students complete the Day 3 activities on page 100. You may want to do the first one as a group.

DAY 4

various
(adj.) More than one kind; several. *I would like to have various shoes to wear for different kinds of weather.*

variety
(noun) A number of different things in a group. *I was amazed by the variety of pens sold in the store.*

Display an array of writing tools. Say: *I have several kinds of things to write with. I have various writing tools to choose from.* Ask students to find other objects in the classroom of which there are **various** kinds. Have them use the word **various** to describe them. Then explain that the word **variety** could also be used. Give an example. Say: *I have various writing tools. I have a variety of writing tools.* Then have students complete the Day 4 activities on page 100. You may want to do the first one as a group.

DAY 5

Have students complete page 101. Call on students to read aloud their answers to the writing activity.

Day 1 vary

1. How would you complete this sentence? Say it aloud to a partner.

I think _____ is boring because it does not vary enough.

2. Which phrase means the opposite of *vary*? Circle your answer.

    a. change in some way

    b. become different

    c. differ from the usual

    d. stay the same

3. Tamara likes to *vary* her hairstyle every week. What does that mean? Circle your answers.

    a. Tamara braids her hair the same way every week.

    b. Tamara's hair might be straight one week, curly the next, and in braids the next.

    c. Tamara does not like to change the way she wears her hair.

    d. Tamara is always looking for different ways to wear her hair.

Day 2 variation

1. How would you complete this sentence? Say it aloud to a partner.

As a variation to our daily routine, I suggest we _____.

2. In which situations would *variation* <u>not</u> be a good idea? Circle your answers.

    a. The rockets can be launched only when certain steps are done in the right order.

    b. The art students were encouraged to use their imaginations.

    c. To compare the results, the experiment must be done the same way each time.

    d. The coach suggested that the team try some new plays.

3. The teacher tells you to copy some sentences from the board with no *variations*. What should you do? Circle your answer.

    a. write the sentences in your own words

    b. write the sentences exactly as they appear

    c. leave out the verbs in the sentences

    d. copy only the sentences that need no changes

Daily Academic Vocabulary

Name _____

Day 3 variation

1. How would you complete this sentence? Say it aloud to a partner.

I would like a variation of _____.

2. Which sentence does not use *variation* correctly? Circle your answer.

   a. That was the best variation of "The Star-Spangled Banner" I have ever heard.

   b. I needed two buttons exactly alike, so I bought these variations.

   c. My uncle's variation of macaroni and cheese includes tomato sauce.

   d. The artist used a slightly different color for each variation of the painting.

3. Which phrase best describes a *variation*? Circle your answer.

   a. a slightly different form   c. a brand new idea

   b. an exact copy   d. an old way

Day 4 various • variety

1. How would you complete these sentences? Say them aloud to a partner.

Because I really like _____, I wish I could own various kinds of them.

A healthy diet includes a variety of _____.

2. Chet's teacher says he must use *various* resources to do his science report. What should he do? Circle your answer.

   a. be sure he changes the topic several times

   b. include different types of sentences throughout the report

   c. be sure to use only an encyclopedia as his source of information

   d. use magazines, Web sites, an encyclopedia, and a book during his research

3. Match each group to the *variety* of items you could find in it. Write the correct letter on the line.

Groups	Item
___ fruits	a. potatoes, beans, squash
___ vegetables	b. tea, lemonade, water
___ drinks	c. lemons, oranges, berries
___ pizza toppings	d. sausage, cheese, pepperoni

Daily Academic Vocabulary

Day 5 vary • variation • various • variety

Fill in the bubble next to the correct answer.

1. **Which reason might be given for *varying* the way something is done?**

　Ⓐ It's good to do things in the same way.

　Ⓑ There is no reason to do it differently.

　Ⓒ You might find a better way to do it.

　Ⓓ Change is never a good thing.

2. **The coach includes plenty of *variation* in the team's daily practices. What does that mean?**

　Ⓕ Players do the same drills every day.

　Ⓖ Players never have to learn new ways of practicing.

　Ⓗ Players always know what to expect next.

　Ⓙ Players practice skills in different ways each day.

3. **Which word means the same as *various*?**

　Ⓐ identical

　Ⓑ several

　Ⓒ change

　Ⓓ single

4. **Which of these sentences does <u>not</u> describe a *variation*?**

　Ⓕ I added extra hot sauce to Grandpa's chili recipe.

　Ⓖ This drawing of the barn looks nothing like the others.

　Ⓗ Each photograph in the series had one small change.

　Ⓙ Each cheerleader tied her bow in a slightly different way.

There is a **variety** of answers to choose from!

Writing An old saying is, "*Variety* is the spice of life." Describe what you think this saying means. Be sure to include the word *variety* in your answer.

_____

_____

_____

_____

project

Use the reproducible definitions on page 181 and the suggestions on page 6 to introduce the words for each day.

DAY 1

project
(noun) A task or planned piece of work that requires much time and effort to complete. *The voters said yes to the building* **project** *for a new stadium.*

Ask students to think about something outside of school that they worked on over time to complete. Say: *When you spend time and effort doing something, you can call it a* **project**. Discuss **projects** happening in your town or city, such as large building **projects**, events, or festivals. Ask: *What is a* **project** *you have worked on outside of school?* Then have students complete the Day 1 activities on page 103. You may want to do the first one as a group.

DAY 2

project
(noun) A school assignment that is completed over a period of time. *Our teacher gave us two weeks to complete our science* **project**.

Remind students that a project is something that takes time and effort to complete. Ask: *What school* **projects** *have you done?* See if students can describe **projects** they have been assigned in various subject areas. Ask: *What makes a* **project** *successful?* Then have students complete the Day 2 activities on page 103. You may want to do the first one as a group.

DAY 3

project
(verb) To stick out farther than or beyond something. *A waterfall is formed from water flowing over rocks that* **project** *from the cliff.*

Go to a bookshelf and pull out one of the books slightly. Say: *This book is* **projecting** *out from the shelf. I need to push it back in.* Write the word "**project**" and its pronunciation on the board. (prō ject′) Point out that it is spelled the same as the word from Days 1 and 2, but it is pronounced differently. Ask: *What are things that* **project**, *or stick out, from the walls in our classroom?* (e.g., clock; shelves; flag) Then have students complete the Day 3 activities on page 104. You may want to do the first one as a group.

DAY 4

project
(verb) To try to figure out ahead of time; to look ahead. *The weather reporters* **project** *lots of rain over the next week.*

Ask students if they pay attention to weather reports. Say: *Weather reporters try to* **project** *the weather. They try to figure out what the weather will be like in the future. What do you* **project** *the weather will be tomorrow?* Then ask: *If I place a pencil on the very edge of my desk, what do you* **project** *will happen? If you work hard and study for a test, what do you* **project** *will happen?* Then have students complete the Day 4 activities on page 104. You may want to do the first one as a group.

DAY 5

Have students complete page 105. Call on students to read aloud their answers to the writing activity.

Day 1 project

1. How would you complete this sentence? Say it aloud to a partner.

I would like to help on a project to _____.

2. Which phrase would not be used to describe a project? Circle your answer.

    a. takes time to finish   c. can be done quickly

    b. requires effort   d. should be carefully planned

3. Which sentences describe projects? Circle your answers.

    a. After seven months, the new theater was finally complete.

    b. The table and chairs were delivered in one shipment.

    c. Every morning we make our beds and help prepare breakfast.

    d. Each board was cut by hand, nailed in place, and given three coats of paint.

4. What is a project you have completed at home?

_____

_____

Day 2 project

1. How would you complete this sentence? Say it aloud to a partner.

My favorite school project ever was _____.

2. Which of these school assignments should not be called a project? Circle your answer.

    a. Read Chapter 10 and answer the questions at the end.

    b. Choose a book, read it, and then create a poster with a summary and an illustration.

    c. Find and conduct a science experiment that you can do at home during spring break.

    d. Cut out 100 different things to use in creating an art mosaic.

3. Which way of working would not be helpful if you were working on a school project? Circle your answer.

    a. Planning something that you should do each day or week.

    b. Putting effort into every step.

    c. Keeping a checklist to show your progress.

    d. Beginning the work the day before it is due.

**Daily
Academic
Vocabulary**

Day 3 | project

1. How would you complete this sentence? Say it aloud to a partner.

Things that project from a building are _____.

2. Which of these things *projects* from something else? Circle your answer.

a. words in a book

b. a scarecrow's long, pointy nose

c. peanut butter in a jar

d. the lines on a piece of notebook paper

3. Which phrase could replace the word *project* in this sentence? Circle your answer.

When you build something, never allow nails to project from the wood.

a. stick out   c. split apart

b. get stuck   d. look different

Day 4 | project

1. How would you complete this sentence? Say it aloud to a partner.

I project that in the summer I will _____.

2. Which of these can you *project*? Circle your answer.

a. what happened yesterday

b. who wrote a book

c. when you will finish writing a story

d. your teacher's name

I **project** that parrots will one day rule the world.

3. Which of these might scientists *project*? Circle your answers.

a. how many people will be on Earth in 50 years

b. how many people live on Earth right now

c. whether humans will be able to live underwater

d. whether humans have walked on the moon

4. What is something you *project* will happen next year?

_____

_____

    Daily Academic Vocabulary • EMC 2760 • © Evan-Moor Corp.

Daily Academic Vocabulary

Day 5 project

Fill in the bubble next to the correct answer.

1. Which definition fits the use of *project* in this sentence?
My whole family works every year on the city library's fundraising project.

- Ⓐ planned work that takes time and effort
- Ⓑ long-term school assignment
- Ⓒ to stick out
- Ⓓ to look ahead

2. Which pair of phrases best describe a school *project*?

- Ⓕ can be done in a day; has steps to follow
- Ⓖ can be complicated; quick to complete
- Ⓗ done over time; requires planning
- Ⓙ lasts all year; don't have to turn it in

3. A travel brochure describes a beach town as having a pier that *projects* half a mile into the ocean. What does that mean?

- Ⓐ You can see the pier from half a mile away.
- Ⓑ The pier was built so that it goes a half mile out into the ocean.
- Ⓒ People are planning to build a very long pier in the future.
- Ⓓ Many people are working to build a big pier in the town.

4. Why might a shoe store owner *project* how many pairs of each type of shoe she will sell?

- Ⓕ because she enjoys doing interesting math problems
- Ⓖ because she likes to know which pairs are sticking out on the shelves
- Ⓗ because she is only interested in past sales
- Ⓙ because she wants to know how many pairs to have in her store

Writing Describe what makes school *projects* interesting to you. For example, do you like to work alone or in a group? In which subject area do the most fun *projects* occur? Be sure to use the word *project* in your writing.

_____

_____

_____

illustrate • illustration
graphic

Use the reproducible definitions on page 182 and the suggestions on page 6 to introduce the words for each day.

DAY 1

illustrate
(verb) To explain or make clear by using examples, stories, or comparisons. *The forest rangers **illustrate** the importance of fire safety by telling stories about huge fires caused by careless campers.*

Say: *Sometimes when I want to help you understand something better, I might use a story or example to **illustrate** what I'm talking about. I take you through the steps, explain the process, and do several example problems. That is how I **illustrate** in math.* Ask: *What could you say to **illustrate** that someone is a good friend? A bad friend?* Then have students complete the Day 1 activities on page 107. You may want to do the first one as a group.

DAY 2

illustrate
(verb) To draw or provide pictures for a book or other written material. *We will **illustrate** the book report by designing our own cover for the book.*

Say: *When artists create pictures for a book or a certain piece of writing, we say they **illustrate** the book or piece of writing.* Have a number of fictional books on hand. Ask students to identify the illustrators of the books. For each book ask: *Who **illustrated** this book?* Then have students complete the Day 2 activities on page 107. You may want to do the first one as a group.

DAY 3

illustration
(noun) A picture someone has created in a book or other written material. *The **illustration** looked so real that I thought it was a photograph.*

Display several books with **illustrations**. Say: *The word **illustration** is also used to name a picture or drawing that someone has created for a book.* Have several students find **illustrations** in the displayed books. Have them tell the class, "I found an **illustration** of ___ in this book." Be sure to differentiate an **illustration** from a photograph. Then have students complete the Day 3 activities on page 108. You may want to do the first one as a group.

DAY 4

graphic
(noun) A picture, diagram, or other image. *Carlos used **graphics** to illustrate his project.*

(adj.) Having to do with pictures or images. *Use a **graphic** organizer to plan your story.*

Say: *A **graphic** is any picture or image. Can you find any **graphics** in our room?* Help students identify **graphics**. Then say: *We also use the word **graphic** to describe something that uses images. For example, we use **graphic** organizers in class. What makes them **graphic** organizers?* (They are images used to organize information.) *How do they use **graphics** to help us organize information?* Encourage students to use the word **graphic**. Then have students complete the Day 4 activities on page 108. You may want to do the first one as a group.

DAY 5

Have students complete page 109. Call on students to read aloud their answers to the writing activity.

Name_____

Day 1 illustrate

1. **How would you complete this sentence? Say it aloud to a partner.**

   My teacher illustrated the importance of how to _____ by _____.

2. **Which of these things might a speaker use to *illustrate* her points? Circle your answers.**

   a. personal stories or examples
   b. a good topic sentence
   c. an unrelated story
   d. facts and figures

3. **Chan's teacher has asked him to *illustrate* rounding a number to the nearest 10. What should he do? Circle your answer.**

   a. draw a big number 10
   b. give a number and explain how he would round it to the nearest 10
   c. tell a story about trying to do something 10 times
   d. count to 100 by 10s

Day 2 illustrate

1. **How would you complete this sentence? Say it aloud to a partner.**

   I think it would be fun to be the artist who illustrates _____.

2. **If an artist is at work *illustrating* something, what is he or she doing? Circle your answer.**

   a. creating pictures to match written words
   b. drawing whatever comes to mind
   c. turning an object into art
   d. writing captions to go with pictures

3. **The company that is going to print a new book wants someone to *illustrate* it. What type of person will the company hire? Circle your answer.**

   a. a songwriter
   b. an artist
   c. an author
   d. a salesperson

4. **Describe how you would *illustrate* a new cover for your favorite book.**

   _____

   _____

   _____

Day 3 | illustration

1. How would you complete this sentence? Say it aloud to a partner.

An illustration in a book I read recently showed _____.

2. Which word should <u>not</u> be used instead of *illustration*? Circle your answer.

a. photograph   c. picture

b. drawing   d. image

3. Which phrases describe *illustrations*? Circle your answers.

a. paintings hanging in a museum

b. pictures in a children's storybook

c. drawings in a magazine article

d. photographs in a newspaper

Day 4 | graphic

1. How would you complete these sentences? Say them aloud to a partner.

Computer graphics help me to _____.

I think a graphic designer is someone who _____.

2. What does a *graphic* presentation do? Circle your answer.

a. tells you how to draw something

b. provides pictures for a book

c. shows information through photographs

d. shows information using images

3. Which of these does <u>not</u> show a *graphic* organizer? Circle your answer.

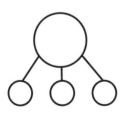   

a.   b.   c.   d.

Name_____

Day 5 illustrate • illustration

Fill in the bubble next to the correct answer.

1. Which word means the same as *illustrate* in this sentence?

The scientist compared the dinosaur with a large bird to illustrate her ideas.

Ⓐ draw

Ⓑ explain

Ⓒ write

Ⓓ list

2. When an artist *illustrates* a book, what does he or she do?

Ⓕ draws pictures for the book

Ⓖ explains the book in words

Ⓗ tries to sell the book

Ⓙ adds color to the book

3. Where would you expect to find an artist's *illustration*?

Ⓐ on a radio show

Ⓑ in a hospital

Ⓒ in a book

Ⓓ at a photography studio

4. *Graphics* are often seen on _____.

Ⓕ trees

Ⓖ your teacher

Ⓗ libraries

Ⓙ Web sites

I'm an illustration!

Writing   How do you use *graphic* organizers in school? How do they help you? Use at least one of this week's words in your description.

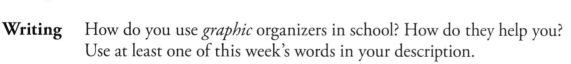

_____

_____

_____

_____

describe • description
descriptive • convey

Use the reproducible definitions on page 183 and the suggestions on page 6 to introduce the words for each day.

DAY 1

describe
(verb) To create a picture of something in words. *I can describe exactly what her dress looks like.*

description
(noun) A spoken or written account of something. *Her description of the restaurant included its sights, smells, and sounds.*

Choose a classroom object and ask students to **describe** it. Say: *Imagine that someone has never seen this. How can you describe it? Use words to create a picture of how it looks and what its purpose is.* Using students' suggestions, work as a class to create a brief **description** of the object. Explain: *Once you figure out how to describe something, you can write a description of it.* Point out that you can **describe** events as well as people, places, and things. Ask for a **description** of students' favorite events. Then have students complete the Day 1 activities on page 111. You may want to do the first one as a group.

DAY 2

descriptive
(adj.) Using or full of description. *My book on Italy is very descriptive.*

Say: *Sometimes you are asked to write a descriptive sentence or paragraph. This means writing something that has a lot of detail.* Ask: *What types of words would you expect descriptive writing to include?* Elicit from students that **descriptive** writing uses adjectives and precise nouns and verbs. Help students make a simple sentence more **descriptive**. (The dog barked.) Then have students complete the Day 2 activities on page 111. You may want to do the first one as a group.

DAY 3

convey
(verb) To take or carry from one place or person to another. *My great-great-grandparents would convey their notes to each other by horseback.*

Call a student forward and say: *(Name), please convey this pen to (another student's name).* Explain that **convey** is another word for "take" or "carry." Ask: *What do ships and trucks convey?* (products from one place to another) *Mail carriers?* (letters) *Trains, planes, and buses?* (passengers) Then have students complete the Day 3 activities on page 112. You may want to do the first one as a group.

DAY 4

convey
(verb) To make known or express. *A poem can convey the poet's feelings about the topic.*

Say: *Convey is also used to talk about making ideas or feelings known to others. A poet conveys a lot of meaning with just a few words. You convey your feelings when you make them known to others.* Ask: *How do people often convey their feelings?* Then have students complete the Day 4 activities on page 112. You may want to do the first one as a group.

DAY 5

Have students complete page 113. Call on students to read aloud their answers to the writing activity.

Daily
Academic
Vocabulary

Day 1 describe • description

1. How would you complete these sentences? Say them aloud to a partner.

If asked to describe my home, I would say _____.

Descriptions of foods should include _____.

2. Which of these things can you <u>not</u> describe? Circle your answer.

a. a recent trip you took

b. how you felt when you did something fun

c. the plot of a book you just read

d. a famous statue you have never seen

3. Write a description of your bedroom.

_____

_____

Day 2 descriptive

1. How would you complete this sentence? Say it aloud to a partner.

When I write, I use descriptive words to _____.

2. Which things would you expect to find in a piece of descriptive writing? Circle your answers.

a. lots of details   c. plain language

b. many adjectives   d. just facts

3. Which of these sentences tell about someone using descriptive words? Circle your answers.

a. The secretary of the club called roll to see who had come to the meeting.

b. As Beth told about her ride on a camel, we all felt like we were there with her.

c. The teacher walked us through the steps in long division.

d. With fewer than 50 words, the poet brought the scene to life.

4. What makes a good piece of descriptive writing?

_____

_____

Name_____

Day 3 | convey

1. How would you complete this sentence? Say it aloud to a partner.

The best way to convey people over long distances is _____.

2. In the world of transportation, which words mean the same as *convey*? Circle your answers.

    a. carry   c. halt

    b. damage   d. deliver

3. In which sentence can the word "carries" be replaced by the word *conveys*? Circle your answer.

    a. My voice carries a long distance as it echoes through the cave.

    b. The bus carries the hotel guests from the airport.

    c. The store carries my favorite brand of chocolate syrup.

    d. In *The Wizard of Oz,* Dorothy carries out her plan to return to Kansas.

Day 4 | convey

1. How would you complete this sentence? Say it aloud to a partner.

When I'm sorry for what I have done, I try to convey that by _____.

2. Which word could replace *convey* in this sentence? Circle your answer.

I decided to convey my appreciation by writing a thank-you note.

    a. handle   c. regret

    b. express   d. transport

3. Carmen's teacher gives her a word-problem assignment and says Carmen should *convey* her answer on paper. What should Carmen do? Circle your answer.

    a. tell her teacher the answer

    b. walk up to the teacher's desk to tell her the answer

    c. write down her answer to the word problem

    d. work with several other students to find the answer

4. What are some words or phrases you would use to *convey* a strong opinion about something?

_____

_____

_____

Name_____

Day 5 describe • description • descriptive • convey

Fill in the bubble next to the correct answer.

1. **You go to the doctor because you have been sick for a few days. The doctor asks you to *describe* how you are feeling. What should you do?**

   Ⓐ draw a picture of yourself feeling ill

   Ⓑ tell a story about a time when you felt sad

   Ⓒ tell the doctor about what is bothering you

   Ⓓ ask the doctor to take your temperature

2. **Which piece of writing probably would <u>not</u> include any *descriptions*?**

   Ⓕ a poem about roses

   Ⓖ a school supply list

   Ⓗ a travel article about Alaska

   Ⓙ a newspaper story about the county fair

3. **A teacher asks different students to do jobs for her. Which job involves *conveying* something?**

   Ⓐ Erase everything from the chalkboard.

   Ⓑ Feed the gerbil.

   Ⓒ Organize the art supplies.

   Ⓓ Take a note to the principal.

4. **If you are *conveying* your happiness, what are you doing?**

   Ⓕ sharing your good feelings

   Ⓖ carrying your feelings inside your heart

   Ⓗ asking others if they are happy

   Ⓙ frowning at other people

Writing   Choose an object in your classroom. Try to *describe* it without naming the object. Underline the words that you think are especially *descriptive*.

_____

_____

_____

_____

CUMULATIVE REVIEW
WORDS FROM WEEKS 19–26

consult
convey
describe
description
descriptive
design
designed
discuss
discussion
display
exhibit
graphic
illustrate
illustration
introduce
introduction
introductory
project
reveal
variation
variety
various
vary

Days 1–4

Each day's activity is a cloze paragraph that students complete with words or forms of words that they have learned in weeks 19–26. Before students begin, pronounce each word in the box on the student page, have students repeat each word, and then review each word's meaning(s). **Other ways to review the words:**

- Start a sentence containing one of the words and have students finish the sentence orally. For example:

  *I like to eat a **variety** of snacks, including…*
  *My friends and I often **discuss**…*

- Provide students with a definition and ask them to supply the word that fits it.

- Ask questions that require students to know the meaning of each word. For example:

  *Why do artists **exhibit** their work?*
  *Why can't one thing be described as **various**?*

- Have students use each word in a sentence.

Day 5

Start by reviewing the words in the crossword puzzle activity for Day 5. Write the words on the board and have students repeat them after you. Provide a sentence for one of the words. Ask students to think of their own sentences and share it with a partner. Call on several students to share their sentences. Follow the same procedure for the remaining words. Then have students complete the crossword activity.

Extension Ideas

Use any of the following activities to help integrate the vocabulary words into other content areas:

- Have students **design** their own Web pages, or help you **design** yours. This can be done on paper and then made digitally. Encourage them to think of **introductory** pages and text, as well as **illustrations** and **descriptions**.

- Have students keep a list of the **various** vehicles they see used to **convey** goods within their community. **Discuss** where the goods are going.

- Assign students a **descriptive** piece of writing. Encourage them to work on grabbing the readers' attention in the **introductory** paragraph. Remind them to use vivid words throughout the piece to make their **descriptions** come to life.

Name_____

Daily Academic Vocabulary

describe	displayed	illustrate	introduction	revealed	various
discussed	graphics	illustrations	project	variation	

Day 1

Fill in the blanks with words from the word box.

Last summer was the first time I had ever seen fossils. My _____

to these clues to the past came at La Brea Tar Pits in California. My family and I

listened to a talk about the three million fossils that were discovered there. The

scientist _____ with us the many animals that lived there in the past.

Enormous elephants called mammoths and huge cats with seven-inch-long teeth were

some of the _____ animals. She had _____, or

drawings, of many of them. She even _____ real mammoth fossils on

a table. I will never forget that trip!

Day 2

Fill in the blanks with words from the word box.

Everyone in class was assigned a _____ for math. We had to

use examples to _____ ways math is used in everyday life. I used

words and _____ to _____ how people have to

add, subtract, and divide to buy things at the store. Gabe showed a different side

of math. His _____ of the project showed how math is used when

playing music. He told the class that music is divided into beats. There are different

kinds of notes that represent a certain number of beats or a fraction of a beat. He

_____ that you must know how to use fractions to count the beats

and play the notes correctly.

Daily Academic Vocabulary

consulted	design	discussion	introduced	varied
convey	designed	exhibit	introductory	variety

Day 3

Fill in the blanks with words from the word box.

One day, Mrs. Gonzales and her class talked about where food came from. The

_____ made the class realize how much work went into making

everything they ate. The class was so interested that Mrs. Gonzales decided to

start something new. She _____ the idea of a school garden. The

class was excited and began to plan. The garden _____ included

a _____ of fruits and vegetables. The food grown would be used

to make a lunch for the class. Several months passed. The garden was a huge

success. The class set up an _____ in the cafeteria to show the

rest of the school how they made their lunch.

Day 4

Fill in the blanks with words from the word box.

Mario read the first few words of the instructions. The _____

paragraph was hard to understand. The model airplane was meant to be a copy of

a real plane and wasn't _____ to fly. But that didn't make it easier

to put together! He stared at the unpainted wood and then went to get advice. He

_____ his grandfather, who expressed excitement in helping. His

grandfather didn't usually _____ so much emotion. Once they

finished gluing and painting, the model plane _____ from a real

plane in only one way. It was 48 times smaller!

Name_____

Day 5

Crossword Challenge

For each clue, write one of the words from the word box to complete the puzzle.

| convey |
| describe |
| description |
| descriptive |
| designed |
| discuss |
| discussion |
| exhibit |
| illustrate |
| introductory |
| reveal |
| vary |

Down

1. Please don't ___ the ending!

3. at the beginning of something

4. to draw

5. a detailed account

Across

2. meant for a special purpose

6. to talk over

7. bring writing to life with ___ words

8. to give details about something

9. to carry

10. to display something for viewing

11. opposite of "stay the same"

12. a serious talk

relate • related
compare • contrast

Use the reproducible definitions on page 184 and the suggestions on page 6 to introduce the words for each day.

DAY 1

relate
(verb) To tell a story or describe an event. *My aunt and uncle will* **relate** *the stories of their travels to us during dinner.*

Explain that when someone describes something that has happened, we can use the verb **relate**. Ask: *Have I* **related** *to you the story of why I became a teacher? What stories do older people in your family like to* **relate**? Then have students complete the Day 1 activities on page 119. You may want to do the first one as a group.

DAY 2

relate
(verb) To make or show a connection between things or people. *I can always* **relate** *my grades to my effort.*

related
(adj.) Having a connection or relationship. *Algebra and geometry are* **related** *subjects in school.*

Remind students that relate can mean the same as "tell." Then explain that **relate** can also mean making a connection between things. Say: *Some people connect the weather to how they feel. For example, some people* **relate** *a happy mood to sunny weather. Others* **relate** *5 o'clock to dinnertime. When things are* **related***, they are connected somehow.* Have students use **relate** and **related** in sentences that follow this pattern: "I **relate** ___ to ___. These two things are **related**." Then have students complete the Day 2 activities on page 119. You may want to do the first one as a group.

DAY 3

compare
(verb) To point out how things are alike and unlike. *In social studies, we* **compare** *the different regions of the world.*

contrast
(verb) To compare in order to show differences. *My report will* **contrast** *today's space flights with early trips into space.*

Say: *While* **compare** *means to point out how things are alike and unlike, we often use* **compare** *in school only to point out how things are alike. So when we are asked to* **compare** *and* **contrast** *things, we tell how they are alike and unlike. When we* **contrast** *things, we only tell how they are different. Let's* **compare** *and* **contrast** *two objects.* Have students choose two objects in the room, or choose two stories you have read recently. Write the words "**compare**" and "**contrast**" in a T-chart on the board. Help students **compare** and **contrast** the two items. Finally, have students complete the Day 3 activities on page 120. You may want to do the first one as a group.

DAY 4

contrast
(noun) A large difference between two things or people. *The huge* **contrast** *in how the two brothers look and act is amazing to me.*

Explain that when pronounced this way, **contrast** is a noun. Say: *What is the* **contrast** *between a weekday and a Saturday? What is the* **contrast** *between light and dark, and between teachers and students? You can talk about* **contrasts** *between people, things, or events.* Then have students complete the Day 4 activities on page 120. You may want to do the first one as a group.

DAY 5

Have students complete page 121. Call on students to read aloud their answers to the writing activity.

Daily Academic Vocabulary

Day 1 relate

1. How would you complete this sentence? Say it aloud to a partner.

I'd like to relate an interesting story about the time I _____.

2. Lian just took her first trip on a train. She will *relate* the details of it in class tomorrow. What should the students expect? Circle your answer.

    a. Lian will write an article about the history of trains.

    b. Lian will tell about what she experienced on her trip.

    c. Lian will have a relative come to speak to the class.

    d. Lian will ask the teacher questions about trains.

3. Which word could be used instead of *related* in this sentence? Circle your answer.

The park ranger related how the lost hikers were found and rescued.

    a. described   c. liked

    b. exaggerated   d. visited

Day 2 relate • related

1. How would you complete these sentences? Say them aloud to a partner.

When I think of a farm, I relate it to _____.

When I'm in a really good mood, it is often related to _____.

2. If you *relate* two ideas to each other, how could you describe them? Circle your answers.

    a. quite serious   c. very strange

    b. connected somehow   d. tied together

3. Which of these activities are *related* to school? Circle your answers.

    a. parent-teacher meetings   c. restaurant grand opening

    b. family reunion   d. fourth-grade field trip

4. How is *Daily Academic Vocabulary* related to your school subjects?

_____

_____

Day 3 compare • contrast

1. How would you complete these sentences? Say them aloud to a partner.

When I compare science and social studies, I find they are alike in _____.

It would be interesting to contrast old and new ways of _____.

2. When you only *compare* two things, what are you looking for? Circle your answers.

   a. all the facts about them   c. ways they are alike
   b. information on how to fix them   d. ways they are different

3. You read an article about two breeds of dogs. Which question asks you to *contrast* them? Circle your answer.

   a. What two kinds of dogs are discussed in this article?
   b. How are they alike?
   c. How are they different?
   d. What do they have in common?

4. *Compare* and *contrast* a sunset and a sunrise.

Compare	Contrast

Day 4 contrast

1. How would you complete this sentence? Say it aloud to a partner.

The biggest contrast between last year at school and this year is _____.

2. Which phrase best describes a *contrast*? Circle your answer.

   a. an interesting idea   c. the same thing
   b. a loud argument   d. a big difference

3. What is the *contrast* between the weather in Alaska and the weather in Florida?

_____

_____

Day 5 relate • related • compare • contrast

Fill in the bubble next to the correct answer.

1. Tiffany is *relating* her adventures at the fair. What is she doing?

Ⓐ feeling sorry for having missed going to the fair

Ⓑ taking her relatives to the fair

Ⓒ connecting the fair to an adventure story she read

Ⓓ telling about her experiences at the fair

How are you and I **related**?

2. Which word could replace *related* in this sentence?

I believe the two scientists' ideas are somehow related.

Ⓕ different

Ⓖ valuable

Ⓗ connected

Ⓙ dangerous

3. If it is easy to *compare* two things, what is probably true about them?

Ⓐ They are very different from each other.

Ⓑ They are alike in many ways.

Ⓒ You like both things equally.

Ⓓ You see the two things all the time.

4. Which sentence *contrasts* two things?

Ⓕ Today's Arctic explorers face many of the same hardships as early explorers.

Ⓖ The Arctic is the frozen region around the North Pole.

Ⓗ Early boats were often crushed by ice, but today's boats can cut through the ice.

Ⓙ Temperatures in the Arctic average ⁻30° in the winter.

Writing A famous saying about differences is, "The *contrast* is like night and day." Why does that make sense? Be sure to use the word *contrast* in your writing.

_____

_____

_____

_____

Daily Academic Vocabulary

explore • exploration
investigate • investigation

Use the reproducible definitions on page 185 and the suggestions on page 6 to introduce the words for each day.

DAY 1

explore
(verb) To travel to a place to discover what it is like. *We will **explore** several caves in the area with a guide.*

Write the names of the continents on the board. Ask: *Which continent would you like to **explore**? If you could travel across a continent learning all about it, which one would you choose? Why?* Then have students complete the Day 1 activities on page 123. You may want to do the first one as a group.

DAY 2

explore
(verb) To consider or think carefully about an idea or possibility. *We should **explore** the different choices we have before deciding.*

Say: *You don't always have to travel in order to **explore** something. You can **explore** by using your mind. When you **explore** something with your mind, you think carefully about an idea or what could happen. People often say they are "**exploring** their options" when they are thinking through an idea.* Have students name choices they made after **exploring** their possibilities. Then have students complete the Day 2 activities on page 123. You may want to do the first one as a group.

DAY 3

exploration
(noun) The act of looking into something closely or studying something unknown. *During our month-long **exploration** of the life cycle, we will watch caterpillars become butterflies.*

Explain that in both uses of "explore," the act of exploring is called an **exploration**. Say: *If you travel to explore, you are on an **exploration**. If you explore ideas by thinking, that is also an **exploration**. What would you like to explore?* Write "Travel Explorations" and "Thinking Explorations" in a T-chart on chart paper. Save the chart for the next lesson. Have students suggest **explorations** of both types. Then have students complete the Day 3 activities on page 124. You may want to do the first one as a group.

DAY 4

investigate
(verb) To look into something closely in order to find out as much as possible about it. *We will **investigate** which rocks are least likely to erode.*

investigation
(noun) The act of investigating. *Our **investigation** of snakes will last two weeks.*

Say: *When people **investigate** something, they look at it very closely. An **investigation** is usually not as open-ended as an exploration. For example, while exploring Antarctica, the scientist decided to **investigate** to find out how deep the ice is. The scientist's exploration was about the whole continent, but her **investigation** was to find out one fact.* Post the T-chart from Day 3. Then ask students to choose an exploration and tell what they would like to **investigate**. What **investigation** could they conduct? Then have students complete the Day 4 activities on page 124. You may want to do the first one as a group.

DAY 5

Have students complete page 125. Call on students to read aloud their answers to the writing activity.

Daily Academic Vocabulary • EMC 2760 • © Evan-Moor Corp.

Day 1 explore

1. **How would you complete this sentence? Say it aloud to a partner.**

   The place I would most like to explore is _____ because _____.

2. **Why might someone want to *explore* a place? Circle your answer.**

   a. to prove that it doesn't exist

   b. to invent a way of getting there

   c. to discover what it is like

   d. to learn about other explorers

3. **Parts of the Grand Canyon can be *explored* only on foot or by horseback. What does that mean? Circle your answer.**

   a. Some trails are only 12 inches wide.

   b. Wild horses are the only animals inside the park.

   c. Drivers must be on the lookout for hikers.

   d. You can travel to see some areas only by walking or riding a horse.

Day 2 explore

1. **How would you complete this sentence? Say it aloud to a partner.**

   When I am interested in an idea, I usually explore it more by _____.

2. **Parents have been *exploring* different ways to raise money for a team's uniforms. What does that mean? Circle your answer.**

   a. The parents have been thinking about different ideas for making money.

   b. The parents have been walking long distances to raise money.

   c. The parents have been learning about how uniforms are made.

   d. The parents have been trying to talk the team out of buying uniforms.

3. **Every night, the Jones family is *exploring* different places to go on their vacation. What are they doing? Circle your answer.**

   a. traveling nightly to look at vacation spots

   b. searching for ideas about good vacations and discussing them

   c. drawing maps to show where they have traveled

   d. refusing to look at more than a couple of vacation ideas

4. **How could you *explore* ideas for a science project?**

   _____

   _____

**Daily
Academic
Vocabulary**

Day 3 exploration

1. How would you complete this sentence? Say it aloud to a partner.

Someday, I would like to take part in an exploration of _____.

2. Which of these sentences does <u>not</u> describe an *exploration*? Circle your answer.

   a. Mieko is studying different resources to learn more about making her own paper.

   b. Several people used flashlights to look at every inch of the strange boulder.

   c. A small group is traveling around the island admiring the unusual flowers.

   d. As Emilio boarded the bus, he wondered if anything surprising would happen today.

3. Which phrase best defines an *exploration?* Circle your answer.

   a. a map showing the details of a place

   b. a careful study of a place or idea

   c. a person who travels the world in search of something

   d. an encyclopedia of topics

4. What do you think you would learn from an *exploration* of a cave?

_____

_____

Day 4 investigate • investigation

1. How would you complete these sentences? Say them aloud to a partner.

I would like to investigate _____.

To do a scientific investigation, you need _____.

2. Which of these workers *investigate* things as part of their jobs? Circle your answers.

   a. police detective   c. research scientist

   b. bank teller   d. bus driver

3. Which statement about an *investigation* is true? Circle your answer.

   a. An investigation is a search for details about a topic.

   b. An investigation takes a brief look at many topics.

   c. An investigation is usually done quickly.

   d. An investigation is for finding big ideas, not details.

Name_____

Day 5 | explore • exploration
investigate • investigation

Fill in the bubble next to the correct answer.

1. If someone wants to *explore* his options, what does he want to do?

Ⓐ to revisit areas that he loves

Ⓑ to move as quickly as possible through an option

Ⓒ to think about all the choices he can make

Ⓓ to choose one option without thinking

2. Which of these is true of the early *explorations* of North America?

Ⓕ The land was unknown to those on the explorations.

Ⓖ Everything was familiar to the people on the explorations.

Ⓗ The explorations were like vacations for travelers.

Ⓙ The explorations stopped when the ships landed.

3. Which word could be used instead of *investigating* in this sentence?

Scientists are investigating the reasons for increased hurricane activity.

Ⓐ choosing

Ⓑ denying

Ⓒ suggesting

Ⓓ studying

4. Which sentence does <u>not</u> describe an *investigation?*

Ⓕ For several weeks, the detectives searched for more clues.

Ⓖ The actress worked daily to memorize her lines.

Ⓗ The scientist read hundreds of articles already written on the topic.

Ⓙ Grandfather spent years tracing the history of our ancestors.

Writing Identify a place or an idea you would like to *explore*. What type of *exploration* would be most helpful? Use the words *explore* and *exploration* as you write.

_____

_____

_____

_____

Daily Academic Vocabulary

WEEK
30

review • preview

Use the reproducible definitions on page 186 and the suggestions on page 6 to introduce the words for each day.

DAY 1

review
(verb) To study or look over something again. *I must carefully review chapters 4 and 5 for the test tomorrow.*

Ask: *How do you get ready for a test?* Listen for the word "**review**," and write it on the board. Discuss that one way to study is to **review** what you have learned. Draw a line to separate the prefix "re-" from the base word "view." Say: *If "view" means "to look at" and "re-" means "again," then review means ____.* Then have students complete the Day 1 activities on page 127. You may want to do the first one as a group.

DAY 2

review
(noun) The act of looking over something again. *A quick review of my test answers showed me that I had skipped a question.*

Say: *Let's do a quick review of multiplication. What is 4 times 3? 5 times 5? What is an easy way to multiply by 10?* Explain that this **review** of multiplication had students go back over what they have already learned. Then have students complete the Day 2 activities on page 127. You may want to do the first one as a group.

DAY 3

review
(verb) To write a report about the strengths and weaknesses of something. *The critic must review new movies and rate them weekly.*

(noun) A report on the strengths and weaknesses of something. *One review of my favorite summer movie said that it was boring.*

Explain to students that when they write a book report, they **review** a book. A **review** tells what is good and bad about the book. Say: *We could call a book report a book review. Newspapers and magazines often print very short book reports called book reviews. Critics also review movies, plays, and restaurants.* Show samples of different **reviews**, if possible, or give your own. Ask: *Why are reviews helpful to other people? Why would others want to read them?* Then have students complete the Day 3 activities on page 128. You may want to do the first one as a group.

DAY 4

preview
(verb) To show or see ahead of time. *About 100 people will preview the play the night before it opens on Broadway.*

(noun) A showing of something ahead of time. *The theater showed a preview of the next movie.*

Remind students of the Day 3 discussion about "review." Then say: *Sometimes people get a "sneak peek" at a movie or a restaurant before it opens for everyone. We say they are previewing, rather than reviewing, when this happens.* Point out the prefix "pre-," meaning "before." Discuss how moviegoers **preview** new movies all the time. Ask: *What previews have you seen? What made them previews?* Then have students complete the Day 4 activities on page 128. You may want to do the first one as a group.

DAY 5

Have students complete page 129. Call on students to read aloud their answers to the writing activity.

126

Daily Academic Vocabulary • EMC 2760 • © Evan-Moor Corp.

Daily
Academic
Vocabulary

Day 1 review

1. **How would you complete this sentence? Say it aloud to a partner.**

    I get the best results when I review for a test by _____.

2. **The speaker always *reviews* her notecards just before she makes a speech. What does she do? Circle your answer.**

    a. writes a new beginning and ending

    b. reads through what she plans to say

    c. tears up her notes so no one can copy them

    d. files the notes in a new way

3. **If you are *reviewing* something, which statement is true? Circle your answer.**

    a. You have seen it before.

    b. It's new and exciting.

    c. You are wasting your time.

    d. You are having your first look at it.

Day 2 review

1. **How would you complete this sentence? Say it aloud to a partner.**

    I think a review of _____ would help me in school.

2. **When Mike is reading his science textbook, he likes to do a *review* of what he has learned after each page. Why is that a good idea? Circle your answer.**

    a. There aren't usually pictures on every page.

    b. It's easier to understand and remember a few ideas at a time.

    c. Reading ahead just a little bit keeps him interested.

    d. His eyes get less tired.

3. **Doing a quick *review* of your answers before turning in a test is a good idea. Why? Circle your answers.**

    a. You can see if you made any mistakes in what you wrote.

    b. You can write down your first thoughts, which are often the best ones.

    c. You can learn new information as you write.

    d. You can see if you skipped any questions.

4. **How can you *review* for a vocabulary quiz?**

    _____

    _____

Day 3 review

1. How would you complete these sentences? Say them aloud to a partner.

I would like to be a critic who reviews _____.

When I write a book review, I include _____.

2. A magazine wants to hire someone to *review* books. What should the person be able to do? Circle your answers.

   a. read forward and backward
   b. see the good and bad parts of a book
   c. turn books into movie scripts
   d. express ideas well in writing

3. Which kinds of information must be in any student *review* by the teacher? Circle your answers.

   a. where the student sits   c. what the student needs to improve
   b. what the student does well   d. what the student eats for lunch

Day 4 preview

1. How would you complete these sentences? Say them aloud to a partner.

It would be exciting to be invited to preview a _____.

What I don't like about movie previews is _____.

2. Which sentence uses the word *preview* correctly? Circle your answer.

   a. We will preview the book after everyone finishes reading it.
   b. A few people were invited to preview the restaurant by dining there before it opened.
   c. We could not preview the movie until after it had been in theaters for a while.
   d. Critics always preview plays after the shows close.

3. What does the prefix "pre-" tell you about when a *preview* occurs? Circle your answer.

   a. before   c. again
   b. after   d. later

4. Write about something you might *preview* in class.

_____

Daily Academic Vocabulary

Day 5 review • preview

Fill in the bubble next to the correct answer.

1. Which phrase describes the <u>opposite</u> of what you do when *reviewing* something?

   Ⓐ looking at something again

   Ⓑ figuring out what something means

   Ⓒ seeing something for the first time

   Ⓓ reading something rapidly

Review your vocabulary words every night!

2. What is the job of a person who *reviews* plays?

   Ⓕ writing about what is good and bad about the play

   Ⓖ making sure the audience has a good view

   Ⓗ listening to the actors memorize their lines

   Ⓙ figuring out how to sell more tickets

3. When are students most likely to do a *review* of information?

   Ⓐ at the beginning of a book

   Ⓑ during computer lab

   Ⓒ when learning something for the first time

   Ⓓ before a test

4. Why might people think an invitation to a *preview* is special?

   Ⓕ because they get to do a favorite activity again

   Ⓖ because they get to see something before others do

   Ⓗ because it is free entertainment

   Ⓙ because they already know so much about it

Writing   Write a short *review* of *Daily Academic Vocabulary.* Be sure to use the word *review* in your writing.

_____

_____

_____

_____

series • process
sequence • sequential

Use the reproducible definitions on page 187 and the suggestions on page 6 to introduce the words for each day.

DAY 1

series
(noun) A group of related things that occur in a row or follow in order. *The author wrote a series of books set in the 1800s.*

Ask: *How many of you are familiar with the* Harry Potter *books? What about* A **Series** of Unfortunate Events? *Each is a series of books. The authors wrote the books with the same characters. It's best to read them in order, from the first book to the last.* Ask: *What are some television shows, movies, or other books that are series?* Say: *The word series can be used to describe anything that follows an order, such as a series of questions.* Have students complete the Day 1 activities on page 131. You may want to do the first one as a group.

DAY 2

process
(noun) A series of actions that produce a result. *Adopting a pet from the animal shelter is not a difficult process.*

Talk with students about the writing **process**, using whatever names you prefer for the different steps. Explain that good pieces of writing result from a **process**, a certain series of actions, not from just sitting down and writing. Ask: *What are other activities that have the best results when a certain process, or series of steps, is followed?* (baking; science; learning) Then have students complete the Day 2 activities on page 131. You may want to do the first one as a group.

DAY 3

sequence
(noun) The order that a series of things or events follows. *The steps must be done in the right sequence for the experiment to work.*

On the board, draw four boxes large enough to write a sentence in. Draw arrows connecting each box with the next. Ask students to relate in **sequence** events from a familiar story. Say: *This chart shows the sequence of events in the story. It shows the order in which the events occurred: what happened first, second, third, and so on.* Then have students complete the Day 3 activities on page 132. You may want to do the first one as a group.

DAY 4

sequential
(adj.) Following a particular order. *The seasons of the year always follow a sequential order.*

Review the definition of "sequence" from Day 3. Then say: *The word sequential is used to describe something that follows a sequence, or order. For example, the events in a story can be described as sequential because they occur in an order.* Ask: *What else can be described as sequential? What do we do in class that is sequential?* Then have students complete the Day 4 activities on page 132. You may want to do the first one as a group.

DAY 5

Have students complete page 133. Call on students to read aloud their answers to the writing activity.

   Daily Academic Vocabulary • EMC 2760 • © Evan-Moor Corp.

Daily
Academic
Vocabulary

Day 1 series

1. How would you complete this sentence? Say it aloud to a partner.

I think a great series of books for kids could be written about _____.

2. Which sentence does not describe a *series*? Circle your answer.

a. Each month, the magazine includes many different articles.

b. The author has written eight books about the triplets' adventures.

c. Television viewers have followed the doctor's life for six seasons now.

d. The next board game from the company will look the same but have new question cards.

3. Which of these describes a *series* of actions? Circle your answer.

a. Chase sat down, went to basketball practice, woke up, and had a dream.

b. Colin finished his homework, turned it in, and went back to his desk.

c. Mirabel asked her teacher to repeat the directions.

d. Suri found her favorite spot in the library to read.

Day 2 process

1. How would you complete this sentence? Say it aloud to a partner.

The best process for cleaning a room is to _____.

2. Which statements are true about a *process*? Circle your answers.

a. You can't be sure what might happen next.

b. Actions should occur in a certain order.

c. You plan for something specific to happen at the end.

d. The order of events is not important.

3. Which school assignment would not require you to follow a *process*? Circle your answer.

a. Follow the directions on page 40 of your science book to make a volcano.

b. Be sure to turn in every stage of your writing project for a grade.

c. Show your work for each step in solving the math problem.

d. Be creative as you think of something to share about the topic of friendship.

4. What are the steps of the writing *process*?

_____

_____

Name_____

Day 3 sequence

1. How would you complete this sentence? Say it aloud to a partner.

I can explain the sequence of events that led to _____.

2. Why is understanding *sequence* important when you read a story? Circle your answer.

   a. You should always keep the setting in mind.

   b. If you don't get to know the characters, you can't understand their actions.

   c. You need to keep track of the order of events.

   d. Main ideas usually are found at the beginnings of paragraphs.

3. Complete this number *sequence*.

68, 70, _____, _____, 76, 78, _____

Day 4 sequential

1. How would you complete this sentence? Say it aloud to a partner.

Something I do in sequential order is _____.

2. Which groups of objects would you expect to be arranged in a *sequential* way? Circle your answers.

   a. trees in a forest   c. apples in a basket

   b. library books on a shelf   d. musical notes in a song

3. Which of these is another way of saying that things are *sequential*? Circle your answer.

   a. They are messy.   c. They are in order.

   b. They are carefully made.   d. They are in pairs.

4. Number the butterfly's life cycle in *sequential* order.

_____   _____   _____   _____

Day 5 series • process • sequence • sequential

Fill in the bubble next to the correct answer.

1. Which of these is <u>not</u> true of things in a *series*?

Ⓒ They are related in some way.

Ⓓ They follow one after another.

Ⓔ They look exactly the same.

Ⓕ You can put them in order.

2. Which of these do people do to complete a *process*?

Ⓕ follow steps to get a certain result

Ⓖ invent a new way of doing things

Ⓗ work quickly without a plan

Ⓘ never produce a result

3. Which of these can display a *sequence* of events?

Ⓒ a number line

Ⓓ a timeline

Ⓔ a line of people

Ⓕ a thought web

My morning
process begins
with a shower.

4. Which set of words is in *sequential* order?

Ⓕ turtle, emergency, pumpkin

Ⓖ car, tires, gas

Ⓗ letters, numbers, sounds

Ⓘ breakfast, lunch, dinner

Writing   Describe the *process* that you follow to get ready for school. Include
the *series* of actions that you take. Use at least one of this week's words
in your writing.

_____

_____

_____

_____

alter • alteration
adapt • adaptation

Use the reproducible definitions on page 188 and the suggestions on page 6 to introduce the words for each day.

DAY 1

alter
(verb) To change or make different. *Our coach will **alter** the game plan at halftime.*

alteration
(noun) A change made to something. *With just a small **alteration** in length, the pants will fit me.*

Ask: *If you change something, what are you doing?* Accept students' correct definitions of "change," and then explain that the word **alter** means the same as "change." The two words are synonyms. Have students use the word **alter** in sentences. Then say: *The way something is **altered** or changed is called an **alteration**. For example, I **altered** my speech by cutting six lines. The **alteration** keeps the speech within the time limit.* Ask: *What **alterations** have you made to school projects?* Then have students complete the Day 1 activities on page 135. You may want to do the first one as a group.

DAY 2

adapt
(verb) To change something for a particular use or purpose. *My aunt will **adapt** her spare bedroom to serve as a home office.*

Ask: *How could we **adapt** this classroom to make it more appropriate for kindergarten students? When I say we should **adapt** the room, I mean we should change it just for this purpose.* Encourage students to use the phrase, "I would **adapt** this classroom by ___." Then have students complete the Day 2 activities on page 135. You may want to do the first one as a group.

DAY 3

adapt
(verb) To become used to new or different conditions. *She **adapted** to the extreme heat of a desert summer.*

Say: *Raise your hand if you have ever moved in your life.* Then say: *Moving is a big change. Any big change means that you have to get used to, or **adapt** to, what is new and different. When you **adapt**, you get used to a change. What did you have to **adapt** to when you moved? What was new or different?* Then have students complete the Day 3 activities on page 136. You may want to do the first one as a group.

DAY 4

adaptation
(noun) A change made for a particular purpose. *An **adaptation** by the anglerfish helps it attract prey in the dark ocean.*

Say: *Some animals make **adaptations**, or changes, in order to get along better in their environment. One example of these **adaptations** might be to turn white in winter. What other animal adaptations can you think of?* Then say: *Remember the changes we talked about to make our room better for a kindergarten class? Those changes were **adaptations**.* Have students complete the Day 4 activities on page 136. You may want to do the first one as a group.

DAY 5

Have students complete page 137. Call on students to read aloud their answers to the writing activity.

Name_____

Day 1 alter • alteration

1. How would you complete these sentences? Say them aloud to a partner.

Actors can alter the way they look by _____.

If I could, I would make an alteration to my _____.

2. Which phrases mean the opposite of *alter*? Circle your answers.

   a. change slightly
   b. change a lot
   c. leave the same
   d. not change

**3. Which sentence does <u>not</u> describe someone making an *alteration*?
Circle your answer.**

   a. To make the jacket shorter, he cut off the bottom and hemmed it.
   b. The cook was careful to make each pancake the same size.
   c. The artist decided to add more clouds to the sky of her painting.
   d. Just before the curtain went up, the actor decided to change his opening lines.

4. How would you like to *alter* your classroom?

_____

Day 2 adapt

1. How would you complete this sentence? Say it aloud to a partner.

I wish I could adapt one room in my home and make it a _____.

2. Which sentence uses the word *adapt* correctly? Circle your answer.

   a. Sari wants to adapt a kitten from the shelter.
   b. You need a special adapt to plug that fan into the wall.
   c. We could adapt the car without making any changes to it.
   d. We hope to adapt the recipe to feed more people.

**3. A music teacher asks her students to *adapt* a song into a short story.
What should they do? Circle your answer.**

   a. Take the words of a song and write a short story that tells the same tale.
   b. Insert a good song into their favorite short story.
   c. Write a song describing their favorite short story.
   d. Write a short story that could be sung.

Day 3 | adapt

1. How would you complete this sentence? Say it aloud to a partner.

It can be hard to adapt to a new school because _____.

2. Which sentence mentions a person who is having to *adapt*? Circle your answer.

   a. Every Friday, Luis visited his grandparents after school.

   b. Carla's first day in middle school was exciting, but also confusing.

   c. Freddy couldn't believe it was already Sunday night.

   d. Wednesday was Jen's favorite day because she had pizza for lunch.

3. Which of these can cause people to *adapt*? Circle your answers.

   a. a new situation   c. a change in plans

   b. a daily routine   d. a regular system

Day 4 | adaptation

1. How would you complete this sentence? Say it aloud to a partner.

I think that the most amazing adaptation by a plant or animal is _____.

2. Cranes are large birds that live in wet areas. Which sentence about cranes does <u>not</u> describe an *adaptation*? Circle your answer.

   a. Cranes have long legs so they can wade through the water.

   b. Cranes have a sharp bill so they can dig up small plants to eat.

   c. Cranes fly long distances to find places to feed.

   d. Cranes have been symbols of peace and long life.

3. Which of these describes an *adaptation*? Circle your answer.

   a. Mei was not able to walk up the steps, so her school built a ramp for her.

   b. Shawna planted the flowers three feet apart.

   c. Duncan thought the movie was too long.

   d. Jayne thought about writing a new song for her sister.

4. Draw an *adaptation* for people so they can live underwater.

Name_____

Day 5 alter • alteration • adapt • adaptation

Fill in the bubble next to the correct answer.

1. If people *alter* what they believe about something, what has happened?

Ⓐ They have said their beliefs very loudly.

Ⓑ They have promised to never change their minds.

Ⓒ They have changed their way of thinking.

Ⓓ They have turned their ideas into a story.

2. Which of these is <u>not</u> true about an *alteration*?

Ⓕ It is a change.

Ⓖ It is something brand new.

Ⓗ It shows a difference.

Ⓙ It starts from an original form.

3. Jeff got a part in the school play. He has to *adapt* his voice to sound older. What might he do?

Ⓐ speak in a much lower voice than usual

Ⓑ sing his lines like a famous star

Ⓒ record his dad saying the lines and then just move his lips

Ⓓ speak normally into a microphone

4. Which sentence describes an *adaptation* made by a plant?

Ⓕ Roses have specific names to describe them.

Ⓖ Giant redwood trees grow from tiny seeds.

Ⓗ Corn tastes best when it is eaten right after it is picked.

Ⓙ The Venus' flytrap eats bugs because it can't get enough food from soil.

Writing   Think of a time when you had to *adapt* to a sudden change or new situation. What helped you get used to the change? Write about the *adaptations* you made, using at least one of this week's words.

_____

_____

_____

_____

WEEK 33

note • notes • notice

Use the reproducible definitions on page 189 and the suggestions on page 6 to introduce the words for each day.

DAY 1

note

(noun) A short letter, message, or reminder. *Our teacher sent a note home to remind parents of the open house at school.*

(verb) To write or jot down. *The coach will note which player wants each jersey number.*

Say: *A note is a short written message. What are the different uses of notes?* (to say thank you; to remind people of something) Ask: *What kinds of notes do you write?* Then say: *When you quickly write, or jot down a few words or ideas—something very short—you can say that you are noting something. For example, each morning I note who did not turn in homework. What do you note on paper?* Then have students complete the Day 1 activities on page 139. You may want to do the first one as a group.

DAY 2

notes

(noun) Words, sentences, and phrases written down to help you remember something. *I always take lots of notes when I review for a test.*

Explain that **notes** also names what you write down when you want to remember something. Say: *You can take notes on what you are learning.* Point out that the phrase "take notes" is very commonly used. Ask students what type of things they might take **notes** on. Then have students complete the Day 2 activities on page 139. You may want to do the first one as a group.

DAY 3

note

(verb) To pay attention to. *Note how the kangaroo uses its tail for balance.*

Say: *Sometimes when you note something, you do not write anything down. Rather, you are noting it in your mind by purposely paying attention to it. For example, today I noted the weather so I would know what to wear. I paid attention to the weather. What have you noted today?* Then have students complete the Day 3 activities on page 140. You may want to do the first one as a group.

DAY 4

notice

(verb) To see something or become aware of it. *Ms. Jones will notice that you came in late.*

(noun) A warning or announcement. *The teacher gave us a week's notice of the test.*

Ask: *Did you notice anything unusual on your way to school today? When you notice something, you see it or become aware of it. Unlike the act of noting something, which you do on purpose, noticing means that you weren't really trying to see it.* Then say: *When you give notice, you are giving a warning or making an announcement.* Say: *If I give you notice of a quiz tomorrow, I am telling you to expect a quiz. What other notices could you receive?* Then have students complete the Day 4 activities on page 140. You may want to do the first one as a group.

DAY 5

Have students complete page 141. Call on students to read aloud their answers to the writing activity.

Name_____

Day 1 note

1. How would you complete these sentences? Say them aloud to a partner.

It's nice to send thank-you notes because _____.

I could keep a pen and paper handy so I could note _____.

2. Which commonly used phrase is best for describing a *note*? Circle your answer.

    a. light and fluffy   c. short and sweet

    b. long and involved   d. tried and true

3. When it's time to leave the library, Franco says, "Wait a moment while I *note* the name of this book." Which phrase could he use instead of *note*? Circle your answer.

    a. ask about   c. stare at

    b. jot down   d. try to find

4. Write a *note* to a friend to suggest something to do together on Saturday.

_____

_____

Day 2 notes

1. How would you complete this sentence? Say it aloud to a partner.

I could include _____ in addition to words when I take notes.

2. In one class, students are graded on how well they take *notes*. What does that mean? Circle your answer.

    a. The teacher sees if what the students write down helps them remember lessons.

    b. The teacher carefully watches to see who is passing notes to friends in class.

    c. Students receive bad grades when they copy other people's notes.

    d. Students are expected to write kind letters to several people every week.

3. Which sentence does <u>not</u> describe someone taking *notes*? Circle your answer.

    a. As he did his research, Ben was careful to write what he learned in his own words.

    b. The author sat down at her computer to write the final chapter of the novel.

    c. Lana wrote down the names of characters and what they did as she was reading.

    d. The student used an outline form to record his teacher's main ideas.

Name_____

Day 3 note

1. How would you complete this sentence? Say it to a partner.

When I came to school today, I noted that _____.

2. When you *note* something interesting, what are you doing? Circle your answer.

    a. paying attention to it   c. hiding it from view

    b. pointing it out to everyone   d. making sure it is correct

3. On their nature walk, the guide told the students to *note* sounds made by animals. What should they do? Circle your answer.

    a. write letters to the guide asking about animals on the trail

    b. find and catch every animal they hear

    c. stop to write about any animals they hear

    d. listen carefully for animal sounds and remember them

Day 4 notice

1. How would you complete these sentences? Say them aloud to a partner.

I have noticed that many kids are wearing _____ this year.

Our principal might give us notice that _____.

2. Which sentence describes what happens when you *notice* something? Circle your answer.

    a. You write a page of notes about it.   c. You cause it to happen.

    b. You become aware of it.   d. You look for it.

3. Which sentence does <u>not</u> describe a person giving *notice* about something? Circle your answer.

    a. An ambulance driver turns on the sirens.

    b. The principal announces the rules of the contest.

    c. The speaker opens the speech with a funny story.

    d. A worker says he will leave his job in two weeks.

4. Where have you read a *notice*? What did it say?

_____

_____

Daily
Academic
Vocabulary

Day 5 note • notes • notice

Fill in the bubble next to the correct answer.

1. Which of these is <u>not</u> a *note*?

Ⓐ detailed instructions about how to do something

Ⓑ a brief reminder about a meeting

Ⓒ a thank-you card for a present

Ⓓ an e-mail about your day

2. Carly is a good shopper. She goes to different stores and carefully *notes* the prices of items she wants to buy. Then she can see which price is the best. How does Carly *note* the prices?

Ⓕ She marks the prices on the price tags.

Ⓖ She looks for the prices on the price tags.

Ⓗ She writes the prices down so she can compare them.

Ⓘ She writes an article on how to be a good shopper.

3. Which of these things should you *note*?

Ⓐ a piece of paper

Ⓑ a thank-you card for your coach

Ⓒ a pencil

Ⓓ what time your soccer practice begins

4. Which of these is <u>not</u> a *notice*?

Ⓕ a statement from a woman that she will run for mayor

Ⓖ a postcard from the library about an overdue book

Ⓗ a scary short story that takes place in the mountains

Ⓘ a phone message from a friend that she can't come over

Note to self:
Buy a new
mirror.

Writing   What kind of *notes* do you write? Tell about two times when you wrote *notes*. Use the word *notes* in your writing.

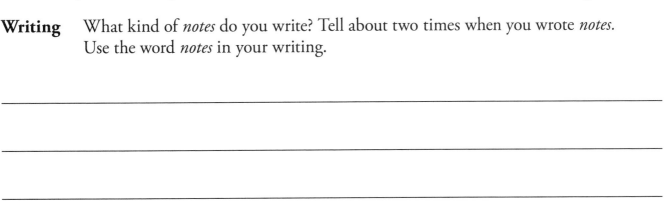

_____

_____

_____

_____

Daily Academic Vocabulary

WEEK 34

reduce • reduction
decrease

Use the reproducible definitions on page 190 and the suggestions on page 6 to introduce the words for each day.

DAY 1

reduce
(verb) To make smaller or less. *Reduce the number of sugary sodas you drink to improve your dental health.*

Ask: *How can we reduce the amount of paper we use? How can we use less paper?* Have students share ideas. Encourage them to use the phrase, "To **reduce** our use of paper, we could ___." Discuss other ways to care for or preserve the environment, using the word **reduce**. Then have students complete the Day 1 activities on page 143. You may want to do the first one as a group.

DAY 2

reduction
(noun) The act of making smaller or decreasing. *A small reduction in speed can lower the amount of gas used by automobiles.*

Say: *When people reduce, the action they are taking is a reduction. For example, the city asks for a reduction in the amount of electricity people use. What does the city want reduced? The government has said there should be a reduction in fatty foods served by schools. What does the government want reduced?* Then ask: *What reductions should our school make?* Then have students complete the Day 2 activities on page 143. You may want to do the first one as a group.

DAY 3

decrease
(verb) To make or become less or smaller. *Water levels in rivers and lakes decrease when rainfall and snowfall are low.*

Point out that one synonym for "reduce" is **decrease**. Say: *If we reduce the amount of paper we use, we decrease our use of paper.* Explain that **decrease** does have one slightly different meaning. Say: *The word decrease is also used when something becomes smaller on its own— that is, without being made smaller by an outside force. For example, we would not say that rainfall "reduces" during a dry season. We would say that rainfall decreases.* Then have students complete the Day 3 activities on page 144. You may want to do the first one as a group.

DAY 4

decrease
(noun) A loss, or the amount by which something becomes smaller. *I see a decrease in my ability to focus in class when I don't get enough sleep.*

Say: *Decrease is also a noun. It is used to describe the amount by which something decreases, or becomes smaller. When you talk about a decrease, you talk about a loss of some sort. For example, a decrease in the temperature of two degrees means the temperature went down by two degrees. What other decreases could we see in terms of weather?* Then have students complete the Day 4 activities on page 144. You may want to do the first one as a group.

DAY 5

Have students complete page 145. Call on students to read aloud their answers to the writing activity.

142

Daily Academic Vocabulary • EMC 2760 • © Evan-Moor Corp.

Name_____

Day 1 reduce

1. How would you complete this sentence? Say it aloud to a partner.

I think I should reduce the amount of time I spend _____ every day.

2. Which phrase fits the meaning of *reduce*? Circle your answer.

    a. to make less important   c. to make larger

    b. to make smaller   d. to figure out

3. If you want to *reduce* the weight of your backpack, what should you do? Circle your answer.

    a. place it on a scale and note its weight

    b. carry it over one shoulder

    c. carry fewer things in it

    d. figure out how to pack more things in it

Day 2 reduction

1. How would you complete this sentence? Say it aloud to a partner.

A reduction in my allowance would probably result in _____.

2. If a principal thanks students for a *reduction* in the amount of trash on school grounds, what is she pleased about? Circle your answer.

    a. The students are leaving less trash around the school.

    b. The students have been using trash cans less often.

    c. The students are bringing more garbage to school.

    d. The students are no longer picking up their trash.

Use a trash can!

3. Why would a *reduction* in pay hurt a worker? Circle your answer.

    a. The worker would have less to do.

    b. The worker would get paid more money for less work.

    c. The worker would become ill.

    d. The worker would earn less money.

4. When can a *reduction* be positive? Give an example.

_____

_____

Day 3 decrease

1. How would you complete this sentence? Say it aloud to a partner.

If the number of students in our school decreased, then _____.

**2. A student says, "My interest in TV has *decreased* since I started reading more."
What has the student done? Circle your answer.**

    a. watched more TV   c. watched TV while reading

    b. watched less TV   d. not watched any TV

**3. If you want to *decrease* the amount of water you use, what should you do?
Circle your answers.**

    a. turn off the water while you brush your teeth

    b. take more showers

    c. dry off completely after your shower

    d. take shorter showers

4. What would you like to *decrease* in your life?

_____

_____

Day 4 decrease

1. How would you complete this sentence? Say it aloud to a partner.

I think a decrease in _____ would be good for my school.

2. Which math equation shows a *decrease* in value? Circle your answer.

    a. $100 - 20 = 80$ c. $3 \times 12 = 36$

    b. $76 + 12 = 88$ d. $14 - 0 = 14$

3. Which sentence tells about a *decrease*? Circle your answer.

    a. Fewer than 50 people came to the concert.

    b. Less than an inch of rain fell yesterday.

    c. More people every year ask for a flu shot.

    d. The number of new band members is much lower this year.

Daily Academic Vocabulary

Day 5 reduce • reduction • decrease

Fill in the bubble next to the correct answer.

1. Which two words mean nearly the same thing?

Ⓐ reduce and shrink

Ⓑ reduce and increase

Ⓒ reduce and know

Ⓓ reduce and lengthen

2. In cooking, a *reduction* is a sauce that is made by getting rid of some of the liquid in the pan. Why does the name make sense?

Ⓕ because the sauce only has one ingredient

Ⓖ because the sauce sounds fancy and needs a long name

Ⓗ because the sauce is finished when there is less liquid

Ⓙ because the sauce is made by adding to the liquid

3. Which of these would cause a *decrease* in an animal's population?

Ⓐ The sun goes down.

Ⓑ The animals eat too much.

Ⓒ It rains.

Ⓓ The animal's habitat is destroyed.

4. A *decrease* is _____.

Ⓕ a gain

Ⓖ a loss

Ⓗ another crease

Ⓙ a death

Writing   Think of something in your community that you would like to see *reduced*. How could people help with this *reduction?* Be sure to use the word *reduce* or *reduction* in your writing.

_____

_____

_____

_____

depend • dependent
independent • independently

Use the reproducible definitions on page 191 and the suggestions on page 6 to introduce the words for each day.

DAY 1

depend
(verb) To be decided or controlled by something else. *Whether we travel on the holidays will depend on the price of gas.*

Say: *Many actions depend on other things. If I told you that the class would have free time if everyone finished their work, then having free time depends on you meeting that goal. The reward is controlled by your behavior. Can you think of other instances when something depends on your actions?* Then have students complete the Day 1 activities on page 147. You may want to do the first one as a group.

DAY 2

depend
(verb) To rely or count on someone or something. *I depend on my alarm clock to wake me up on time.*

Explain that we use "**depend** on" to indicate that we count on something or someone. Say: *I depend on you to ask questions when you don't understand something.* Ask students to use "**depend** on" to describe how they rely, or count, on other people, things, or events. Then have students complete the Day 2 activities on page 147. You may want to do the first one as a group.

DAY 3

dependent
(adj.) Depending on or controlled by someone or something else. *My grades are usually dependent on how much I study.*

independent
(adj.) Not controlled by other people or countries. *Mexico became independent from Spain in 1821.*

Say: *Your grades are dependent on several things: class participation, homework, test scores. How you do in these areas controls your grade.* Ask students to suggest other results in life that are **dependent** on something else. Then ask: *What would it be like to live in a country where your rights were dependent on what a ruler would allow?* Reinforce that it is a great privilege to live in an **independent** country, and what that means to the students. Then have students complete the Day 3 activities on page 148. You may want to do the first one as a group.

DAY 4

independently
(adv.) By yourself. *I am proud when I complete my homework independently.*

independent
(adj.) Not needing support or help from others. *My little sister has become very independent.*

Ask: *Is it better to work independently or as a group?* Talk about the pros and cons of each scenario. Then ask: *When do you think it is good to be independent? By that I mean, when is it admirable not to need help or support from others? Do you consider yourself to be independent? When?* Have students share their ideas, using the word **independent** in their responses. Then have students complete the Day 4 activities on page 148. You may want to do the first one as a group.

DAY 5

Have students complete page 149. Call on students to read aloud their answers to the writing activity.

Name_____

Day 1 depend

1. **How would you complete this sentence? Say it aloud to a partner.**

   Usually what my friends and I decide to do when we're together depends on _____.

2. **Johari's weekly allowance *depends* on if she completes her chores.**
   What does that mean? Circle your answers.

   a. Johari gets an allowance depending upon whether she completes her chores.
   b. Johari has different chores and a different allowance every week.
   c. Johari receives the money when she does not complete any of her chores.
   d. The amount of Johari's allowance is out of her control.

3. **A plant's growth *depends* on water, soil, and the sun. How should you care for a plant?**
   Circle your answer.

   a. Leave it outside at night.
   b. Keep the plant in an underground pool.
   c. Leave it alone.
   d. Make sure it gets sunlight and water when planted in soil.

Day 2 depend

1. **How would you complete this sentence? Say it aloud to a partner.**

   When I am sad, I depend on my _____ to cheer me up by _____.

2. **Each group member *depends* on each of the others to do a good job.**
   That makes which of these statements true? Circle your answer.

   a. Only one of the group members needs to do his or her work.
   b. Each group member must do his or her part for the project to be a success.
   c. Each member's work can be done by someone else.
   d. Only a few of the group members need to do a good job.

3. **Which phrase best replaces *depend* in this sentence? Circle your answer.**

   I depend on my teacher to help me learn new skills.

   a. decide for   c. rely on
   b. dislike for   d. watch for

4. **Who *depends* on you? What does he or she *depend* on you to do?**

   _____

Name_____

Day 3 dependent • independent

1. How would you complete these sentences? Say them aloud to a partner.

I am dependent on _____ for _____.

Because our class is independent from the other fourth-grade classes, we can _____.

2. A group of students knows that their project grade is *dependent* on how much each of them contributes to the work. To get a good grade, what should the students do? Circle your answer.

   a. point out to the teacher which student controlled the project
   b. each try to do better than the other group members
   c. be sure every group member does an important part of the project
   d. complain to the teacher about the decision on how to do the project

3. Which word means the opposite of *independent*? Circle your answer.

   a. controlled   c. lonely
   b. free   d. reliable

I'm free as a bird!

Day 4 independently • independent

1. How would you complete these sentences? Say them aloud to a partner.

One activity I enjoy doing independently is _____.

I can remember feeling very independent the first time I _____ by myself.

2. Which of these activities could <u>not</u> be done *independently*? Circle your answer.

   a. making sandwiches   c. riding a seesaw
   b. reading a book   d. watching a movie

3. A report card describes a student as "a good *independent* worker." What does that mean? Circle your answer.

   a. The student prefers to work with at least one other person.
   b. The student works well alone.
   c. The student is bossy.
   d. The student likes to read silently.

Name_____

Fill in the bubble next to the correct answer.

1. Which of these things does <u>not</u> *depend* on something else?

Ⓐ a play's success

Ⓑ the sun

Ⓒ your health

Ⓓ the height of a tree

2. Kayla's soccer team has a chance of going to the championship game. However, it is *dependent* on another team losing its next game. What does this mean?

Ⓕ Kayla's team can make it to the championship if they try harder.

Ⓖ Kayla's team should not worry about how the other teams are playing.

Ⓗ Kayla's team has lost one too many games.

Ⓙ Kayla's team can move to the championship only if the other team loses.

3. Which words best describe an *independent* country?

Ⓐ not controlled by any other countries

Ⓑ ruled by people who only like their own way of thinking

Ⓒ very far away from any other country

Ⓓ not needing its people to care about government

4. Which sentence correctly uses the word *independently*?

Ⓕ The pier was independently despite the rising floodwaters.

Ⓖ The team had an independently amount of time to finish the project.

Ⓗ In some sports, athletes are able to practice independently.

Ⓙ Jana worked with a partner because she likes to work independently.

Writing   Think of someone or something you *depend* on. Describe this person or thing, using at least one of this week's words.

_____

_____

_____

_____

CUMULATIVE REVIEW
WORDS FROM WEEKS 28–35

adapt
adaptation
alter
alteration
compare
contrast
decrease
depend
dependent
exploration
explore
independent
independently
investigate
investigation
note
notes
notice
preview
process
reduce
reduction
relate
related
review
sequence
sequential
series

Days 1–4

Each day's activity is a cloze paragraph that students complete with words or forms of words that they have learned in weeks 28–35. Before students begin, pronounce each word in the box on the student page, have students repeat each word, and then review each word's meaning(s). **Other ways to review the words:**

- Start a sentence containing one of the words and have students finish the sentence orally. For example:

  *I enjoy hearing people **relate** stories about…*
  *I follow the same **process** every time I…*

- Provide students with a definition and ask them to supply the word that fits it.

- Ask questions that require students to know the meaning of each word. For example:

  *What are some school activities that must be done **independently**?*
  *What tools do detectives use to **investigate** crimes?*

- Have students use each word in a sentence.

Day 5

Start by reviewing the words not practiced on Days 1–4: **independent, independently, notes, preview, reduction, relate, sequence, sequential**. Write the words on the board and have students repeat them after you. Provide a sentence for one of the words. Ask students to think of their own sentence and share it with a partner. Call on several students to share their sentences. Follow the same procedure with the remaining words. Then have students complete the code-breaker activity.

Extension Ideas

Use any of the following activities to help integrate the vocabulary words into other content areas:

- Ask students to name places on Earth they would like to **explore**. Locate each place on a globe and ask students to suggest a list of supplies they would need to take for each **exploration**. **Compare** the lists. Talk about the **contrasts** between the climate and terrain of each place.

- Ask students to **preview** the next book you plan to have them read. Suggest that they take **notes** on their initial reactions to the book.

- Explore the Fibonacci **sequence**. Teach students about patterns found in nature. Have them conduct an **investigation** into the **sequence** in nature.

Name_____

Daily Academic Vocabulary

adaptation	contrasted	explorations	noted	related
compare	depending	investigated	noticed	review

Day 1

Fill in the blanks with words from the word box.

Sequoia (suh-kwoi-uh) trees, the largest trees in the world, have been studied

for years. Scientists' _____ into the lives of these trees show how

they have changed to do well in their environment. One _____

connected to their success is their gigantic size. Their ability to live through cold

winters and strong winds is _____ to their size. Scientists have

also paid attention to and _____ that a sequoia's size is controlled

by a mix of sun, water, and space. _____ on this mix, a sequoia

can grow as tall as a 27-story building and weigh as much as 20 blue whales!

Day 2

Fill in the blanks with words from the word box.

Will's class did a report on the strengths and weaknesses of the Internet.

For their _____, they had to choose two different Web sites

on the same subject. They had to pay attention to how the sites were alike and

_____ them. Will took a close look and _____

two Web sites on the solar system. On one site, he saw that some of the information

was different and _____ with the other site. But he also

_____ that both sites were really easy to use. His report showed

that the Internet is very useful, but that it is a good idea to double-check information.

Name_____

| adapted | altering | dependent | investigation | reduced |
| alteration | decreased | explored | process | series |

Day 3

Fill in the blanks with words from the word box.

My teacher told us that each year a person throws away up to 500 pounds of

garbage. So my class decided to look into recycling. Our _____

showed us that we could get special containers to put paper and aluminum cans in.

Instead of going to a landfill or dump, the paper and cans would be picked up and

go through a number of actions. This _____ would allow them to

be used again. We decided to change our actions by _____ what

we put in the trash. It worked! We _____ our waste. Our garbage

_____ by half!

Day 4

Fill in the blanks with words from the word box.

Sir Ernest Shackleton was a brave man who _____ Antarctica

in 1914. He and 27 other men wanted to be the first to cross the frozen continent,

but they were stopped by a group of occurrences. That _____ of

events began when their ship was crushed by ice and they had to quickly change

their plans. The _____ in the trip involved the crew relying on six

men who went for help. The _____ men had to get used to the new

situation. Luckily, they _____ to the harsh conditions. When the

six men found help, everyone was rescued. It had been two years since they began

their adventure!

Daily
Academic
Vocabulary

Day 5

Crack the Code!

Write one of the words from the word box on the lines next to each clue.

adapt	decrease	independently	preview	review
adaptation	depend	investigate	process	sequence
alter	dependent	investigation	reduce	sequential
alteration	exploration	note	reduction	series
compare	explore	notes	relate	
contrast	independent	notice	related	

1. things written down to help you remember something ___ ___ ___ ___ ___
   $\qquad\qquad\qquad\qquad\quad$ 1 $\qquad$ 2

2. by yourself ___ ___ ___ ___ ___ ___ ___ ___ ___ ___ ___ ___ ___
   $\qquad\qquad\qquad\qquad\qquad\qquad\qquad\qquad\qquad\quad$ 3

3. to see or show ahead of time ___ ___ ___ ___ ___ ___ ___
   $\qquad\qquad\qquad\qquad\qquad\qquad\quad$ 4

4. the act of making smaller ___ ___ ___ ___ ___ ___ ___ ___ ___
   $\qquad\qquad\qquad\qquad\quad$ 5

5. to tell a story ___ ___ ___ ___ ___ ___
   $\qquad\qquad$ 6 $\qquad$ 7

6. one after the other ___ ___ ___ ___ ___ ___ ___ ___ ___ ___
   $\qquad\qquad\quad$ 8 $\qquad\qquad\qquad$ 9

7. the order that a series of events follows ___ ___ ___ ___ ___ ___ ___ ___
   $\qquad\qquad\qquad\qquad\qquad\quad$ 10 $\qquad$ 11

Now use the numbers under the letters to crack the code. Write the letters on the lines below. The words will complete this sentence.

A sequoia can live for _____.

___ ___ ___ ___ h ___ ___ ___ ___ ___ ___ ___ ___ ___ ___
 9 4 1 9 1 10 2 7 11 5 3 8 7 6 2

Answer Key

Week 1

Day 1
2. b
3. Answers will vary.

Day 2
2. d
3. b

Day 3
2. c
3. b, d, c, a

Day 4
2. b
3. d

Day 5
1. C   2. F   3. D   4. G

Week 2

Day 1
2. a, d
3. b

Day 2
2. a, d
3. b

Day 3
2. a
3. a, d

Day 4
2. c
3. c

Day 5
1. B   2. F   3. D   4. G

Week 3

Day 1
2. c
3. a

Day 2
2. a, b
3. b, d

Day 3
2. d
3. a

Day 4
2. b, c
3. a, b

Day 5
1. C   2. J   3. C   4. G

Week 4

Day 1
2. d
3. b, a, d, c

Day 2
2. a
3. b, d

Day 3
2. d
3. Answers will vary.

Day 4
2. a
3. b

Day 5
1. B   2. F   3. B   4. F

Week 5

Day 1
2. b, c
3. c

Day 2
2. a
3. d

Day 3
2. c
3. a, d

Day 4
2. a, d
3. Answers will vary.

Day 5
1. C   2. G   3. A   4. G

Week 6

Day 1
2. b
3. c

Day 2
2. b, c
3. Answers will vary.
4. Answers will vary.

Day 3
2. a, d
3. a
4. Answers will vary.

Day 4
2. c
3. b

Day 5
1. B   2. J   3. A   4. J

Week 7

Day 1
2. a, d
3. d

Day 2
2. c
3. Answers will vary.

Day 3
2. b, d
3. c

Day 4
2. d
3. a

Day 5
1. B   2. F   3. D   4. H

Week 8

Day 1
2. a, d
3. 2, 1, 4, 3

Day 2
2. c, d
3. c

Day 3
2. d
3. b

Day 4
2. a
3. d

Daily Academic Vocabulary • EMC 2760 • © Evan-Moor Corp.

Day 5
 1. C   2. F   3. C   4. J

Review Week 9

Day 1
 segment, identified, rare, frequently, affected

Day 2
 argument, organization, selection, identical, frequency

Day 3
 infrequent, composition, passage, effect, selected

Day 4
 views, argue, organize, outline, compose

Day 5
 Down
 1. affect, 2. argue,
 3. identification, 6. impact,
 7. identical, 8. identify,
 10. rare
 Across
 4. frequent, 5. outline,
 9. section, 11. view,
 12. compose

Week 10

Day 1
 2. b, d
 3. d

Day 2
 2. a, c
 3. c

Day 3
 2. d
 3. d

Day 4
 2. c
 3. c, d, a, b

Day 5
 1. B   2. J   3. A   4. H

Week 11

Day 1
 2. a
 3. b, c

Day 2
 2. d
 3. a, c

Day 3
 2. c
 3. a

Day 4
 2. a
 3. c

Day 5
 1. A   2. H   3. D   4. G

Week 12

Day 1
 2. c
 3. a

Day 2
 2. b, c
 3. d

Day 3
 2. c
 3. c, d, b, a

Day 4
 2. a, c
 3. a

Day 5
 1. A   2. J   3. B   4. H

Week 13

Day 1
 2. b
 3. a

Day 2
 2. d
 3. b

Day 3
 2. a
 3. a

Day 4
 2. b
 3. c

Day 5
 1. B   2. F   3. C   4. H

Week 14

Day 1
 2. d
 3. a, d

Day 2
 2. a
 3. b

Day 3
 2. b, d
 3. c

Day 4
 2. a
 3. c

Day 5
 1. D   2. G   3. A   4. H

Week 15

Day 1
 2. c
 3. a
 4. b

Day 2
 2. b
 3. c

Day 3
 2. b
 3. d

Day 4
 2. a
 3. b
 4. a

Day 5
 1. B   2. H   3. A   4. J

Week 16

Day 1
 2. a
 3. b

Day 2
 2. b
 3. c

Day 3
 2. a
 3. c

Day 4
2. b
3. d
Day 5
1. B   2. H   3. A   4. H

Week 17

Day 1
2. b
3. d
Day 2
2. c
3. a, d
4. b, d
Day 3
2. b, d
3. c, b, d, a
Day 4
2. a
3. c
Day 5
1. C   2. G   3. A   4. J

Review Week 18

Day 1
method, detect, indicating, signals, prompted
Day 2
discovered, resourceful, assembled, methodical, experiences
Day 3
structures, supports, source, resources, responsibility
Day 4
assembly, responsible, indications, detectable, discovery
Day 5
1. background
2. methodical
3. indication
4. responsibility
5. detect
6. assemble
7. prompt
code: dark of the night

Week 19

Day 1
2. a, c
3. b
Day 2
2. b
3. a
Day 3
2. b
3. c
Day 4
2. a
3. d
Day 5
1. B   2. H   3. A   4. J

Week 20

Day 1
2. b
3. b, d
Day 2
2. a, c
3. b, a, d, c
Day 3
2. c
3. d
Day 4
2. c
3. b
Day 5
1. A   2. J   3. A   4. G

Week 21

Day 1
2. c
3. a, d
Day 2
2. b
3. a, b
4. d
Day 3
2. c
3. d
Day 4
2. b, c
3. a

Day 5
1. D   2. G   3. A   4. G

Week 22

Day 1
2. c
3. b, d
Day 2
2. a, c
3. b
4. b, c
Day 3
2. b
3. c, a, d, b
Day 4
2. d
3. b
Day 5
1. C   2. F   3. B   4. J

Week 23

Day 1
2. d
3. b, d
Day 2
2. a, c
3. b
Day 3
2. b
3. a
Day 4
2. d
3. c, a, b, d
Day 5
1. C   2. J   3. B   4. G

Week 24

Day 1
2. c
3. a, d
4. Answers will vary.
Day 2
2. a
3. d
Day 3
2. b
3. a

Daily Academic Vocabulary • EMC 2760 • © Evan-Moor Corp.

Day 4
2. c
3. a, c
4. Answers will vary.
Day 5
1. A   2. H   3. B   4. J

Week 25

Day 1
2. a, d
3. b
Day 2
2. a
3. b
4. Answers will vary.
Day 3
2. a
3. b, c
Day 4
2. d
3. c
Day 5
1. B   2. F   3. C   4. J

Week 26

Day 1
2. d
3. Answers will vary.
Day 2
2. a, b
3. b, d
4. Answers will vary.
Day 3
2. a, d
3. b
Day 4
2. b
3. c
4. Answers will vary.
Day 5
1. C   2. G   3. D   4. F

Review Week 27

Day 1
introduction, discussed,
various, illustrations,
displayed

Day 2
project, illustrate, graphics,
describe, variation, revealed
Day 3
discussion, introduced, design,
variety, exhibit
Day 4
introductory, designed,
consulted, convey, varied
Day 5
Down
1. reveal, 3. introductory,
4. illustrate, 5. description

Across
2. designed, 6. discuss,
7. descriptive, 8. describe,
9. convey, 10. exhibit,
11. vary, 12. discussion

Week 28

Day 1
2. b
3. a
Day 2
2. b, d
3. a, d
4. Answers will vary.
Day 3
2. c
3. c
4. Answers will vary.
Day 4
2. d
3. Answers will vary.
Day 5
1. D   2. H   3. B   4. H

Week 29

Day 1
2. c
3. d
Day 2
2. a
3. b
4. Answers will vary.

Day 3
2. d
3. b
4. Answers will vary.
Day 4
2. a, c
3. a
Day 5
1. C   2. F   3. D   4. G

Week 30

Day 1
2. b
3. a
Day 2
2. b
3. a, d
4. Answers will vary.
Day 3
2. b, d
3. b, c
Day 4
2. b
3. a
4. Answers will vary.
Day 5
1. C   2. F   3. D   4. G

Week 31

Day 1
2. a
3. b
Day 2
2. b, c
3. d
4. Answers will vary.
Day 3
2. c
3. 72, 74, 80
Day 4
2. b, d
3. c
4. 4, 1, 3, 2
Day 5
1. C   2. F   3. B   4. J

Week 32

Day 1
2. c, d
3. b
4. Answers will vary.

Day 2
2. d
3. a

Day 3
2. b
3. a, c

Day 4
2. d
3. a
4. Answers will vary.

Day 5
1. C   2. G   3. A   4. J

Week 33

Day 1
2. c
3. b
4. Answers will vary.

Day 2
2. a
3. b

Day 3
2. a
3. d

Day 4
2. b
3. c
4. Answers will vary.

Day 5
1. A   2. H   3. D   4. H

Week 34

Day 1
2. b
3. c

Day 2
2. a
3. d
4. Answers will vary.

Day 3
2. b
3. a, d
4. Answers will vary.

Day 4
2. a
3. d

Day 5
1. A   2. H   3. D   4. G

Week 35

Day 1
2. a, c
3. d

Day 2
2. b
3. c
4. Answers will vary.

Day 3
2. c
3. a

Day 4
2. c
3. b

Day 5
1. B   2. J   3. A   4. H

Review Week 36

Day 1
explorations, adaptation, related, noted, depending

Day 2
review, compare, investigated, contrasted, noticed

Day 3
investigation, process, altering, reduced, decreased

Day 4
explored, series, alteration, dependent, adapted

Day 5
1. notes
2. independently
3. preview
4. reduction
5. relate
6. sequential
7. sequence
code: two thousand years

Daily Academic Vocabulary • EMC 2760 • © Evan-Moor Corp.

Index

compose

(verb) To be the parts of something; make up.

*Six small squares **compose** the large rectangle.*

composition

(noun) What something is made of.

*The **composition** of our class is more girls than boys.*

compose

(verb) To write or create.

*You should **compose** a thank-you note after receiving a gift.*

composition

(noun) A musical or written work, such as a song or essay.

*Her **composition** won first prize in the state essay contest.*

organize • organization — DAY 1

organize

(verb)	To put together in a neat and orderly way.	*I **organize** my clothes by type and color.*

organization

(noun)	The way in which things are arranged or grouped together.	*The **organization** of the books is by author, not by subject.*

organize — DAY 2

(verb)	To plan and run an event.	*Scout troops **organize** a big cookie sale every year.*

organize — DAY 3

(verb)	To join together, or form, a group of people.	*The players will **organize** a new soccer team this summer.*

organization — DAY 4

(noun)	A group of people joined together for some purpose.	*We formed an **organization** to raise money for a new park.*

rare

(adj.)   Not often seen, found, or happening.

*The scientist searched her whole life for the **rare** plant.*

frequent • frequently

frequent

(adj.)   Happening often.

*His **frequent** smiles brighten everyone's day.*

frequently

(adv.)   Many times; often.

*I **frequently** bring an extra juice drink in my lunch.*

infrequent

(adj.)   Not happening very often.

*The **infrequent** rainfall makes the desert very dry.*

frequency

(noun)   The number of times something happens in a given period of time.

*The **frequency** of forest fires increases during hot weather.*

view
DAY **1**

(noun) An opinion or idea.

*Her **view** is that we shouldn't have to go to school on Fridays.*

view
DAY **2**

(verb) To have a particular opinion or idea.

*We **view** this problem as easy to solve.*

argue
DAY **3**

(verb) To give reasons for or against something.

*Doctors will **argue** that we should eat lots of fruits and vegetables.*

argument
DAY **4**

(noun) A reason given for or against something.

*Their **argument** for a change in school lunches is based on giving kids healthier choices.*

outline

(noun) A line or shape that shows the outer edge of something.

*You can see the **outline** of the lake on the map.*

outline

(verb) To draw the edge or shape of something.

*I decided to first **outline** the tree before I started coloring.*

outline

(noun) A written summary that shows the main points or ideas of something.

*It is a good idea to first do an **outline** before you start writing a report.*

outline

(verb) To give the main points or ideas of something.

*Please listen while I **outline** the plans for our field trip.*

effect

(noun) Something that happens as a result of something else.

*One **effect** of the hot weather is that more people are using the swimming pool.*

affect

(verb) To have an effect on or to change someone or something.

*His illness will **affect** my plans to go to the park on Saturday.*

affect

(verb) To touch the feelings of someone.

*Certain songs always **affect** my mood, making me feel happy or sad.*

impact

(noun) The strong effect that something has on a person or thing.

*The book about ants had an **impact** on how I feel about insects.*

identify • identification

identify

(verb) To show what or who something is.

*She could not **identify** the man in her dream.*

identification

(noun) The act of showing who a person or thing is.

*The **identification** of each plant was the first step in the science experiment.*

identify

(verb) To think of one thing as being connected to another thing.

*I **identify** ice cream with summer.*

identical

(adj.) Exactly alike.

*The mother and daughter sound **identical** on the phone.*

identification

(noun) Something that proves who you are, such as a card with your name and picture on it.

*A passport is the **identification** you need to travel to another country.*

select

(verb) To pick or choose from a group.

*I want to **select** where we will go for our spring trip.*

selection

(noun) The act of picking out or choosing someone or something from a group.

*We made our **selection** from the list of sandwiches.*

(noun) A person or thing that is chosen.

*My **selection** for "best summer book" was* Gertrude Goes to the City.

section • passage

section

(noun) One of the parts that makes up the whole of something.

*Downtown is my favorite **section** of the city.*

passage

(noun) A short section of a written work or a piece of music.

*We were asked to find the **passage** that tells where the story takes place.*

segment

(noun) One of the parts into which a whole is divided.

*One orange **segment** seemed to have all the seeds.*

detect • detectable

detect

| (verb) | To discover or notice. | *I could **detect** the odor of perfume in the empty room.* |

detectable

| (adj.) | Able to be detected; noticeable. | *The officer reported no **detectable** tire tracks on the road.* |

discover

| (verb) | To find or see something before anyone else. | *In my favorite dream, I **discover** a new island.* |

| (verb) | To find out about something. | *At the fair, I **discovered** how much I liked some new foods.* |

discovery

| (noun) | The act of seeing or finding out something for the first time. | *We all look forward to the **discovery** of cures for the world's many diseases.* |

discovery

| (noun) | Something that is seen or found out for the first time. | *Gold was an important **discovery** in California in the 1800s.* |

responsible

(adj.) Expected to do certain jobs or duties.

*We are **responsible** for turning our homework in on time.*

responsibility

(noun) A job or duty.

*Taking care of a pet is a big **responsibility**.*

responsible

(adj.) Being the cause of something.

*The storm was **responsible** for our power going out.*

responsible

(adj.) Able to do things in a dependable and trustworthy way.

*I think she will be a very **responsible** class president.*

experience

(noun)	Something that a person has done or lived through.	*Summer camp was an amazing **experience** that I will never forget.*
(verb)	To live through or undergo.	*Everyone should **experience** the thrill of downhill skiing.*

experience

(noun)	The knowledge or skill gained by doing something.	*Our newest player has lots of **experience** playing goalie.*

background

(noun)	The part of a picture or scene that is behind the main subject.	*I decided to use yellow to color the **background** of my picture.*

background

(noun)	The events and conditions that lead up to or help explain another event or situation.	*The information that the TV reporter gave provided **background** to help viewers understand why the factory closed.*

indicate

| **(verb)** | To point out something clearly. | *Several signs along the way **indicate** where to turn.* |

indicate • indication

indicate

| **(verb)** | To be a sign of something. | *Birds starting to sing can **indicate** that spring is coming.* |

indication

| **(noun)** | Anything that is a sign of something. | *A fever is an **indication** of sickness.* |

signal

| **(noun)** | Any word or action agreed upon as a warning, message, or command. | *A soft tap on the wall was our **signal** that someone was coming.* |

signal

| **(verb)** | To send a signal to someone or something. | *Kirsten **signaled** me by waving her arms.* |

assemble

(verb) To bring or come together in a group.

*Before each game, we **assemble** as a team for a pep talk.*

assembly

(noun) A group of people meeting together for a particular reason.

*An **assembly** for the whole school will be held on Friday.*

assemble

(verb) To put together all the parts of something.

*The twins can **assemble** a kite faster than anyone else I know.*

assembly

(noun) The act of putting parts together to make a whole.

*The **assembly** of the bookshelves took several hours.*

prompt

| **(adj.)** | Quick and without delay; on time. | *Dad is always **prompt** when picking us up after soccer practice.* |

prompt

| **(verb)** | To get someone to do something. | *When my room is messy, my parents **prompt** me to clean it.* |
| **(noun)** | A signal or cue to do something. | *The actor needed a **prompt** when he forgot his lines.* |

method

| **(noun)** | A way in which something is done. | *One **method** to help you remember new words is to say it several times in a sentence.* |

methodical

| **(adj.)** | Done in a careful way that follows a system or plan. | *The **methodical** worker followed the directions step by step.* |

structure

(noun)	Something that has been built, such as a building.	*Nearly every large modern* **structure**, *such as a skyscraper, has steel in it.*
(noun)	The way in which something is organized or put together.	*The* **structure** *of our school day includes time for outside play.*

support

(verb)	To hold something up in order to keep it from falling.	*Stakes* **support** *small trees as they are growing.*

support

(verb)	To believe in something or someone.	*My parents* **support** *the plan to build more classrooms at our school.*
(noun)	The act of providing help and encouragement.	*I was happy to give* **support** *to the class food drive.*

support

(verb)	To show to be true.	*The test results* **support** *my claim that most of the students understand the material.*

source

(noun) The place, person, or thing from which something comes.

*A dictionary is a good **source** for information on the meaning of words.*

resource

(noun) Someone or something that can be turned to for help or support.

*The phone book is a good **resource** for finding somebody's phone number.*

resource

(noun) Something valuable to a person, place, or group of people.

*One **resource** for meeting our energy needs is wind power.*

resourceful

(adj.) Good at knowing what to do or where to get help.

*Our parents taught us to be **resourceful** and make our own lunches.*

Daily Academic Vocabulary

introduce
DAY 1

(verb)   To begin or start.

*The speaker will **introduce** his talk with a funny story.*

introduce • introduction
DAY 2

introduce

(verb)   To bring in something new.

*In the next chapter, the author will **introduce** an unexpected event.*

introduction

(noun)   The first time that something is experienced.

*My uncle gave me my **introduction** to chess.*

introduction
DAY 3

(noun)   The opening part of a book or other written work.

*The book's **introduction** was written by a famous scientist.*

introductory
DAY 4

(adj.)   Serving to introduce.

*The principal opened the assembly with **introductory** remarks about school spirit.*

Daily Academic Vocabulary • EMC 2760 • © Evan-Moor Corp.

reveal

(verb)	To make known or tell.	*I do not like it when people **reveal** the ending of a movie I haven't seen.*

reveal

(verb)	To uncover or bring into view.	*If Grandpa takes off his hat, he will **reveal** his bald head.*

exhibit

(verb)	To show or display something for viewing.	*The art students will **exhibit** their best artwork in the mall.*
(verb)	To show or reveal feelings, behaviors, or signs of something.	*I never **exhibit** my anger in a hurtful way.*

display

(verb)	To put on view or show something.	*We proudly **display** our trophies in a glass case.*
(noun)	Something that is put on view for everyone to see.	*The museum's **display** of old masks is amazing.*

consult

(verb) To go to another person or other source for information or advice.

*My parents always **consult** a doctor when I have a fever.*

discuss

(verb) To talk over something with other people.

*We should **discuss** how we will present our reports.*

discussion

(noun) A serious talk about something.

*I thought our **discussion** about the poem was very interesting.*

discuss

(verb) To present an idea or point of view by writing or talking about it.

*The speaker will **discuss** his ideas for how to improve our school.*

Daily Academic Vocabulary • EMC 2760 • © Evan-Moor Corp.

design

(verb) To draw or plan something that could be built or made.

*As a final social studies project, we will **design** our own energy-saving homes.*

design

(noun) A drawing or plan showing how something is to be built or made.

*Be sure to follow the **design** carefully when putting together the model train tracks.*

designed

(verb) To be meant for a special purpose.

*The sports shirt was **designed** to keep athletes cooler.*

design

(noun) A pattern made up of lines, figures, or objects.

*I used brightly colored squares and circles in my **design**.*

Daily Academic Vocabulary

vary

(verb) To be different or become different from what was before.

*The date of Thanksgiving will often **vary** because the holiday must be on a Thursday.*

variation

(noun) A change from the usual.

*I look forward to the **variation** in my schedule during summer.*

variation

(noun) A slightly different form or version of something.

*The school cafeteria serves a different **variation** of pizza every day.*

various • variety

various

(adj.) More than one kind; several.

*I would like to have **various** shoes to wear for different kinds of weather.*

variety

(noun) A number of different things in a group.

*I was amazed by the **variety** of pens sold in the store.*

project

(noun) A task or planned piece of work that requires much time and effort to complete.

*The voters said yes to the building **project** for a new stadium.*

project

(noun) A school assignment that is completed over a period of time.

*Our teacher gave us two weeks to complete our science **project**.*

project

(verb) To stick out farther than or beyond something.

*The waterfall is formed from water flowing over rocks that **project** from the cliff.*

project

(verb) To try to figure out ahead of time; to look ahead.

*The weather reporters **project** lots of rain over the next week.*

illustrate
DAY 1

| (verb) | To explain or make clear by using examples, stories, or comparisons. | *The forest rangers **illustrate** the importance of fire safety by telling stories about huge fires caused by careless campers.* |

illustrate
DAY 2

| (verb) | To draw or provide pictures for a book or other written material. | *We will **illustrate** the book report by designing our own cover for the book.* |

illustration
DAY 3

| (noun) | A picture someone has created in a book or other written material. | *The **illustration** looked so real that I thought it was a photograph.* |

graphic
DAY 4

| (noun) | A picture, diagram, or other image. | *Carlos used **graphics** to illustrate his project.* |

| (adj.) | Having to do with pictures or images. | *Use a **graphic** organizer to plan your story.* |

describe • description

describe

(verb)   To create a picture of something in words.

*I can **describe** exactly what her dress looks like.*

description

(noun)   A spoken or written account of something.

*Her **description** of the restaurant included its sights, smells, and sounds.*

descriptive

(adj.)   Using or full of description.

*My book on Italy is very **descriptive**.*

convey

(verb)   To take or carry from one place or person to another.

*My great-great-grandparents would **convey** their notes to each other by horseback.*

convey

(verb)   To make known or express.

*A poem can **convey** the poet's feelings about the topic.*

relate

(verb) To tell a story or describe an event.

*My aunt and uncle will **relate** the stories of their travels to us during dinner.*

relate • related

relate

(verb) To make or show a connection between things or people.

*I can always **relate** my grades to my effort.*

related

(adj.) Having a connection or relationship.

*Algebra and geometry are **related** subjects in school.*

compare • contrast

compare

(verb) To point out how things are alike and unlike.

*In social studies, we **compare** the different regions of the world.*

contrast

(verb) To compare in order to show differences.

*My report will **contrast** today's space flights with early trips into space.*

contrast

(noun) A large difference between two things or people.

*The huge **contrast** in how the two brothers look and act is amazing to me.*

explore

(verb) To travel to a place to discover what it is like.	*We will **explore** several caves in the area with a guide.*

explore

(verb) To consider or think carefully about an idea or possibility.	*We should **explore** the different choices we have before deciding.*

exploration

(noun) The act of looking into something closely or studying something unknown.	*During our month-long **exploration** of the life cycle, we will watch caterpillars become butterflies.*

investigate • investigation

investigate

(verb) To look into something closely in order to find out as much as possible about it.	*We will **investigate** which rocks are least likely to erode.*

investigation

(noun) The act of investigating.	*Our **investigation** of snakes will last two weeks.*

review

(verb) To study or look over something again.

I must carefully review chapters 4 and 5 for the test tomorrow.

review

(noun) The act of looking over something again.

A quick review of my test answers showed me that I had skipped a question.

review

(verb) To write a report about the strengths and weaknesses of something.

The critic must review new movies and rate them weekly.

(noun) A report on the strengths and weaknesses of something.

One review of my favorite summer movie said that it was boring.

preview

(verb) To show or see ahead of time.

About 100 people will preview the play the night before it opens on Broadway.

(noun) A showing of something ahead of time.

The theater showed a preview of the next movie.

series

(noun) A group of related things that occur in a row or follow in order.

*The author wrote a **series** of books set in the 1800s.*

process

(noun) A series of actions that produce a result.

*Adopting a pet from the animal shelter is not a difficult **process**.*

sequence

(noun) The order that a series of things or events follows.

*The steps must be done in the right **sequence** for the experiment to work.*

sequential

(adj.) Following a particular order.

*The seasons of the year always follow a **sequential** order.*

alter • alteration — DAY 1

alter

(verb) To change or make different.

*Our coach will **alter** the game plan at halftime.*

alteration

(noun) A change made to something.

*With just a small **alteration** in length, the pants will fit me.*

adapt — DAY 2

(verb) To change something for a particular use or purpose.

*My aunt will **adapt** her spare bedroom to serve as a home office.*

adapt — DAY 3

(verb) To become used to new or different conditions.

*She **adapted** to the extreme heat of a desert summer.*

adaptation — DAY 4

(noun) A change made for a particular purpose.

*An **adaptation** by the anglerfish helps it attract prey in the dark ocean.*

Daily Academic Vocabulary

note
DAY 1

(noun)	A short letter, message, or reminder.	*Our teacher sent a **note** home to remind parents of the open house at school.*
(verb)	To write or jot down.	*The coach will **note** which player wants each jersey number.*

notes
DAY 2

(noun)	Words, sentences, and phrases written down to help you remember something.	*I always take lots of **notes** when I review for a test.*

note
DAY 3

(verb)	To pay attention to.	***Note** how the kangaroo uses its tail for balance.*

notice
DAY 4

(verb)	To see something or become aware of it.	*Ms. Jones will **notice** that you came in late.*
(noun)	A warning or announcement.	*The teacher gave us a week's **notice** of the test.*

reduce

(verb) To make smaller or less.

Reduce the number of sugary sodas you drink to improve your dental health.

reduction

(noun) The act of making smaller or decreasing.

A small reduction in speed can lower the amount of gas used by automobiles.

decrease

(verb) To make or become less or smaller.

Water levels in rivers and lakes decrease when rainfall and snowfall are low.

decrease

(noun) A loss, or the amount by which something becomes smaller.

I see a decrease in my ability to focus in class when I don't get enough sleep.

depend
DAY 1

| (verb) | To be decided or controlled by something else. | *Whether we travel on the holidays will **depend** on the price of gas.* |

depend
DAY 2

| (verb) | To rely or count on someone or something. | *I **depend** on my alarm clock to wake me up on time.* |

dependent • independent
DAY 3

dependent

| (adj.) | Depending on or controlled by someone or something else. | *My grades are usually **dependent** on how much I study.* |

independent

| (adj.) | Not controlled by other people or countries. | *Mexico became **independent** from Spain in 1821.* |

independently • independent
DAY 4

independently

| (adv.) | By yourself. | *I am proud when I complete my homework **independently**.* |

independent

| (adj.) | Not needing support or help from others. | *My little sister has become very **independent**.* |